W9-BZE-297

Martin Classical Lectures

1. *The Martin Classical Lectures,* edited by Louis E. Lord
2. *Aspects of Social Behavior in Ancient Rome,* Tenney Frank
3. *Attic Vase-Painting,* Charles T. Seltman
4. *The Humanistic Value of Archaeology,* Rhys Carpenter
5. *Greek Ideals and Modern Life,* Sir R. W. Livingstone
6. *Five Men: Character Studies from the Roman Empire,* Martin Percival Charlesworth
7. *Early Greek Elegists,* Cecil M. Bowra
8. *The Roman Art of War under the Republic,* F. E. Adcock
9. *Epigraphica Attica,* Benjamin Dean Meritt
10. *Archaic Attic Gravestones,* Gisela M. A. Richter
11. *Greek Personality in Archaic Sculpture,* George Karo
12. *Thucydides and the World War,* Louis E. Lord
13. *Classical Influences in Renaissance Literature,* Douglas Bush
14. *Pindar and Aeschylus,* John H. Finley, Jr.
15. *The Classics and Renaissance Thought,* Paul Oskar Kristeller
16. *Ancient Book Illumination,* Kurt Weitzmann
17. *Boundaries of Dionysus: Athenian Foundations for the Theory of Tragedy,* Alfred Cary Schlesinger
18. *Society and Civilization in Greece and Rome,* Victor Ehrenberg
19. *Aristophanes and the Comic Hero,* Cedric H. Whitman
20. *The Origin and Early Form of Greek Tragedy,* Gerald F. Else
21. *The Meaning of Stoicism,* Ludwig Edelstein
22. *Rubens and the Classical Tradition,* Wolfgang Stechow

Volume XXII

Martin Classical Lectures

The Martin Classical Lectures
are delivered annually at Oberlin College
on a foundation established by his many friends
in honor of Charles Beebe Martin,
for forty-five years a teacher
of classical literature
and classical art in Oberlin.

Rubens and the Classical Tradition

Wolfgang Stechow

Published for Oberlin College
by Harvard University Press
Cambridge, Massachusetts

1968

Distributed in Great Britain by Oxford University Press, London
Library of Congress Catalog Card Number: 68-54025
Printed in the United States of America

Book design by David Ford

TO THE MEMORY OF

Georg Graf Vitzthum von Eckstädt

1880-1945

Preface

The following lectures were conceived for, and addressed to, the audience of the Martin Classical Lectures series—an audience of laymen interested in the classical past and the classical tradition. Thus, it would have been tempting for the present writer to follow the precedent set by a distinguished older author of a layman's book on Rubens, Robert Vischer, in calling this slender volume "ein Büchlein für unzünftige Kunstfreunde" —a booklet for unprofessional lovers of art. It was the author's aim to offer his interpretation of our present knowledge of the subject; the attempt to break new ground in this area of research must be left to Rubens specialists.

The text of the lectures has remained basically unchanged; however, some footnotes and bibliographical references have been included in the printed version, and the art historian may also find the body of illustrations somewhat useful. The last chapter, on the previous literature on the subject from the seventeenth to the twentieth century, was part of the lecture series; it was—and is now—given as a coda rather than an introduction, because it seemed preferable to offer it to a listener or reader already informed about the essential aspects of the problem.

My greatest debt is to Mrs. Laurine Mack Bongiorno, Oberlin, for her untiring help in improving the text. The illustrations have been gathered with the support of many helpers, among whom I should like to mention with particular gratitude: Frans Baudouin, Antwerp; Carlos van Hasselt, Paris; Julius Held, New York; J. Kuznetsov, Leningrad; Richard Spear, Oberlin. George M. A. Hanfmann, Cambridge, Mass., provided valuable information on archaeological literature. To the Harvard University Press go my thanks for the permission to quote extensively from Miss Ruth S. Magurn's exemplary translation and edition of Rubens' letters; I am obliged to the Phaidon Press in London for allowing me to quote from their edition of Jacob Burckhardt's *Recollections of Rubens* (in the translation of M. Hottinger). Other translations are mine unless indicated otherwise.

Finally, I am very grateful to the Committee on the Charles Beebe Martin Lectureship, particularly to its chairman, Professor Charles T. Murphy, for its kind invitation to join the distinguished group of its lecturers.

Wolfgang Stechow

Oberlin, Ohio
April 1968

Contents

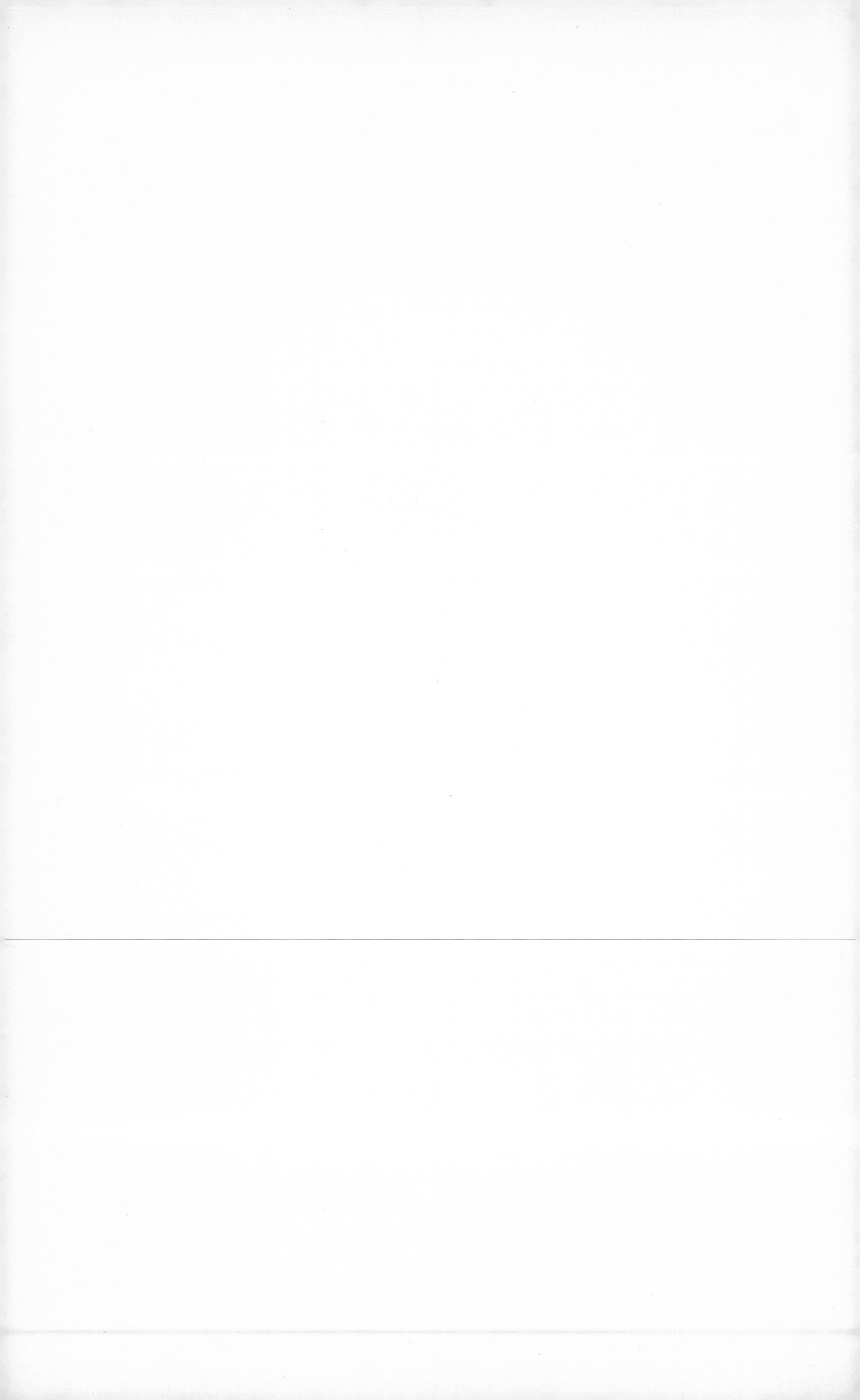

Illustrations

Rubens and the Classical Tradition

Abbreviated Titles

BURCHARD-D'HULST: L. Burchard and R.-A. d'Hulst, *Rubens Drawings,* Antwerp, 1963.

CORRESPONDANCE: *Correspondance de Rubens* (Codex diplomaticus Rubenianus, ed. M. Rooses and Ch. Ruelens, 6 vols., Antwerp, 1887-1909.

EVERS 1942: H. G. Evers, *Peter Paul Rubens,* Munich, 1942.

EVERS 1943: H. G. Evers, *Rubens und sein Werk,* Brussels, 1943.

EXH. AMSTERDAM 1933: *Rubens Tentoonstelling,* Amsterdam: J. Goudstikker, 1933.

EXH. ANTWERP 1956: *Tekeningen van P. P. Rubens,* ed. L. Burchard and R.-A. d-Hulst, Antwerp, Rubenshuis, 1956.

EXH. FOGG-MORGAN 1956: *Drawings and Oil Sketches by P. P. Rubens from American Collections,* ed. A. Mongan, Fogg Art Museum and Pierpont Morgan Library, 1956.

FUBINI-HELD: G. Fubini and J. S. Held, "Padre Resta's Rubens Drawings after Ancient Sculpture;" *Master Drawings,* II (1964), 123ff.

GLÜCK-HABERDITZL: G. Glück and F. M. Haberditzl, *Die Handzeichnungen von Peter Paul Rubens,* Berlin, 1928.

GORIS-HELD: J. A. Goris and J. Held, *Rubens in America,* New York, 1947.

HELD, DRAWINGS: Julius Held, *Rubens, Selected Drawings,* 2 vols., London, 1959.

KDK: Peter Paul Rubens, *Des Meisters Gemälde,* ed. R. Oldenbourg, Stuttgart-Berlin, 1921 (Klassiker der Kunst series).

MAGURN, LETTERS: *The Letters of Peter Paul Rubens,* translated and edited by R. S. Magurn, Cambridge, Mass.: Harvard University Press, 1955.

OLDENBOURG 1922: R. Oldenbourg, *Peter Paul Rubens,* ed. W. von Bode, Munich-Berlin, 1922.

RECOLLECTIONS: Jacob Burckhardt, *Recollections of Rubens,* ed. H. Gerson, trans. M. Hottinger, London: Phaidon Press, 1950.

ROOSES 1904: M. Rooses, *Rubens,* 2 vols., London, 1904.

I. The Literary and Archaeological Heritage

Fully seventy years have passed since the first publication of Jacob Burckhardt's *Erinnerungen aus Rubens,*[1] translated into English as *Recollections of Rubens* in 1950.[2] Like some other great works of the Swiss author, including the *Weltgeschichtliche Betrachtungen,*[3] it was published posthumously; there was no fanfare about it, and there were not even any illustrations. Yet, it is still the greatest book on Rubens, not as a piece of detailed research but as the only all-encompassing guide to that inexhaustible phenomenon which is the life, the personality, and the art of Peter Paul Rubens. The quiet distinction of Burckhardt's literary style, in which every word counts and every thought engenders chains of thought in the attentive reader, can be judged from the first paragraph, which at the same time delineates the scope and tenor of the whole book: "It is an exhilarating task to evoke the life and personality of Rubens; good fortune and kindliness abound in him as in hardly any other great master, and he is well enough known for us to feel sure of our judgment of him. In the consciousness of his own noble nature and great powers he must have been one of the most privileged of mortals. No life is perfect, and trials came to him, too, but the sum of his life so illuminates all its details that, looked at as a whole, it seems exemplary. It did not come to a premature end, like that of Masaccio, Giorgione or Raphael, while on the other hand he was spared the weakness of age, and it was in his last years that he created some of his grandest works. True, from a very early age he met with advancements on all hands, but not everyone could have taken advantage of this and made men and circumstances serve him as Rubens did, with the greatest composure . . . "[4]

And I cannot resist the temptation to quote here, in addition to the first paragraph of this great book, its very last, in which the beautiful description of one of Rubens' landscapes with a classical subject culminates in what to Burckhardt must have signified the highest possible praise for his hero:

"Finally . . . in one of the most splendid pictures in the Pitti Palace, the storm-clouds over the sea are departing and in the heights, a distant, ethereal apparition, we see Pallas in supplication before Jove; soft, warm morning atmosphere occupies the rest of the horizon, and in the most magical light, a mountain rises steeply, with waterfalls, castles and a garden set with terraces and beautiful buildings. These are the gardens of Alcinous, king of the Phaeacians, whose seaport is visible in the distance. In the foreground, we see the ship-wrecked Ulysses, a naked suppliant, for whom Pallas has been interceding with Jupiter, while the king's daughter, whose maids had taken flight before him, quietly orders them to give him help and clothing. It is Nausicaa.

And so they meet, the Ionian and the Fleming, the two greatest story-tellers our earth has ever borne—Homer and Rubens."[5]

What, one is prompted to ask, enabled Jacob Burckhardt, whose name in the mind of most is associated with a series of great studies in the Renaissance, to write the finest of all books on one of the giants of the Baroque? To this question there are two answers, and it is a blessing that these answers are complementary rather than contradictory. It was Burckhardt's compatriot and academic successor, Heinrich Wölfflin, who, about twenty years after the first publication of Burckhardt's book on Rubens, gave us a brilliant and highly influential exposition of the *contrast* between Renaissance and Baroque,[6] and we are still, one is tempted to say, reeling under its impact. It demonstrated the stylistic or, in any case, the formal discrepancies between the art of the early sixteenth and that of the seventeenth century with so much persuasiveness that our eyes have become somewhat dimmed to the recognition of all that which binds the two styles together. For Burckhardt, who was first and foremost a cultural historian, although he was also one of the great art historians of his century, that complete dichotomy did not exist, and we are only slowly beginning to realize how much truth has been jettisoned with the almost total abandonment of his view. The wisdom of his insights has been corroborated by the recent—post-Burckhardtian *and* post-Wölfflinian—recognition of Mannerism as a more or less distinct style *between* High Renaissance and Baroque,[7] a recognition which makes understandable why the masters of the early Baroque, in a natural opposition to the Mannerists, looked back to the High Renaissance for inspiration. Just as Burckhardt, during his late years, realized that Baroque architecture was not a caricature but in a very real sense the logical climax of Renaissance architecture[8] he saw in Rubens the logical climax, the *Vollender,* of Renaissance painting, even though he did not say so explicitly.

But we must not make any unwarranted assumptions. Next to Rubens, Burckhardt's favorite painter of the Baroque was Murillo,[9] whereas he reserved some of his severest criticism for Rembrandt.[10] This clearly indicates that Burckhardt selected his Baroque heroes from among those masters who owed most to Italian Renaissance art; and although today we tend to see, and even to emphasize, a similar relationship between the late Rembrandt and the great masters of the Italian Renaissance, Burckhardt's image of Rembrandt was primarily defined by the high-Baroque and indeed very un-Renaissancelike art of the Dutch master's early years. It would therefore be wrong to think of Burckhardt's concept of, and love for the Baroque as all-inclusive; on the other hand, it is significant that he was by no means, as one might at first suspect, a great admirer of Rembrandt's opposite in Baroque art, Nicolas Poussin. The classical scholar Burckhardt was no classicist. The catholic taste of the modern art historian, which calls for no apology, can be equally attracted to the most serenely balanced compositions of Poussin and the most smashingly high-Baroque performances of Rembrandt; but Burckhardt was primarily attracted by the master who transformed the classical heritage with the greatest measure of spiritual power and artistic independence, and although he failed to see that same quality in the art of Bernini, his conversion to Rubens remains one of the greatest examples of openness of mind and heart ever offered by a scholar reared in the classical tradition.

I have emphasized this point not only because of our eternal debt to a great book but also because my subject requires my posing a typically Burckhardtian question: what do the sources tell us about Rubens' actual knowledge of the classical tradition? Naturally, our ultimate aim will be a discussion of how Rubens *transformed* the classical tradition in his own art, that is, how the classical tradition helped Rubens to become Rubens. But we cannot avoid a fairly detailed report on what this tradition looked like in his time and how much of it was available to him, both in literary and in archaeological terms,—in the form of ancient writing and ancient art.

When we compare the social stratum from which the vast majority of Renaissance and Baroque artists emerged with that of Rubens' family we find it easy to believe Burckhardt's statement that "from a very early age he met with advancements on all hands."[11] His father, Jan Rubens, was a well-known and well-to-do Antwerp lawyer who had taken his doctor's degree in Rome in 1554. Even in his self-imposed exile as a Calvinist he continued to live the life of a gentleman, first in Cologne and later, after his disastrous love affair with the wife of William the Silent of Orange, in near captivity in the town of Siegen in Westphalia, where he was reunited with his faithful and wonderfully forgiving wife, Maria Pypelinckx, and where their son Peter Paul war born on June 28, 1577. Baptized a Lutheran but destined to be a Catholic of indubitable sincerity, the young Rubens spent his first school years in Cologne. When two years after the death of Jan Rubens, which occurred in 1587, his widow returned to Antwerp with her children, Peter Paul, then twelve years old, was placed in the best school in town, together with Balthasar Moretus, who was to become the principal publisher both of Antwerp and of Rubens. Their teacher, Verdonck, taught them Flemish, Latin, and even some Greek. The roster of the books used in this institution included Cicero, Vergil and Terence in Latin, and Plutarch in Greek. This foundation was laid at a time when the young Rubens had not yet begun to dream of becoming a painter.

In the year 1591–92, Rubens served as a page to a noblewoman, Marguerite de Ligne; but by the end of 1592, when he was fifteen, the decision to be an artist had been made. Within six years, he passed through the workshops of three Antwerp painters, among whom Otto van Veen, himself a well-educated man, was the most important. By 1598 Rubens was a master in the guild of St. Luke; but in May, 1600, he departed for Italy, the country in which his father had completed his training as a lawyer and in which his teacher van Veen had completed his training as a painter. Rubens was twenty-three years old, and his artistic output of the preceding period is still insufficiently known; we have difficulty in separating it from van Veen's. Rubens was no prodigy of the kind so brilliantly represented by his greatest pupil, Anthony van Dyck.

To a large extent, the eight years in Italy were still formative years. It is true that by 1603 he had received some fairly important assignments in Mantua, in Spain, and even in Rome; but he did not emerge as a recognized master until the end of those eight years, when he was awarded some really significant Roman commissions. And all the time he never ceased to study and to copy the works of older masters, from classical statues and reliefs to the most recent masterpieces of the nascent Italian Baroque. To this visual heritage, particularly as far as it concerns antiquity, I shall return later; here it is important to remember that these years were also years of increasing knowledge of ancient literature. His position as painter to the court of the Gonzaga in Mantua, to which he was called almost immediately upon his arrival in Italy, was a guarantee of acquaintance not only with the humanists living at that court but also with their colleagues in other centers; to these Rubens had easy access either as a member of the Duke's entourage or as the beneficiary of the very liberal policy of the court in matters of absences for study. As early as 1600 he attended the marriage by proxy of Henri IV of France and Marie de' Medici in Florence and undoubtedly also the performance, which graced that occasion, of the first opera ever presented to a large group and which of course had an antique subject: Jacopo Peri's *Euridice.* With his brother Philip, who like his father took his doctor's degree in Rome and who in spite of his early death attained the rank of a distinguished classical scholar, he visited the sites and doubtless also the libraries of Mantua, Padua, and Verona, and later those of Rome.

The proof of Peter Paul's growing knowledge of the literary classical tradition is found in his letters, an inexhaustible treasure house now made accessible to all in Miss Ruth S. Magurn's excellent English edition.[12] Most of these letters were written in Italian, the rest in French and Netherlandish; they cover the span from 1603 to his death in 1640 and begin with a fascinating series of reports from his important diplomatic mission to Spain, dispatched to his Mantua counselor and friend Annibale Chieppio. His letter of May 24, 1603, written in Valladolid, contains some rather uncomplimentary remarks about several Spanish painters, of whose restorations of a group of damaged pictures that had been left in his care he sharply disapproved. He characterized their work with the first classical quotation we encounter in his letters: "Pergimus pugnantia secum, cornibus adversis componere," which is a free adaptation from Horace's *Sermones* (We continue to fight over opposite viewpoints, with horns directed against each other).[13] As we investigate his later correspondence, we find intermingled with many short Latin expressions of a common sort, partly perhaps of his own making, a plethora of quotations from Plutarch, Cicero, and Vergil (these, it will be recalled, he had already studied in school); Homer, Menander, Euclid and Archimedes, Procopius and Justinian; Plautus, Catullus, Ovid, Petronius, the two Plinys, Valerius Maximus, Juvenal (a favorite), Sallust, Tacitus, Quintus Curtius Rufus and Marcus Aurelius. There is here no trace of showing off, and his familiarity with ancient writers may have been much greater than this selection suggests.

It is true that most if not all subjects of his paintings can be traced to the authors just cited from his letters; but I might add that some of those subjects are very rare, even perhaps unique in the history of art, and betray a close familiarity with the texts before him. Some of these rare subjects I shall consider later; here I shall briefly mention the story of *Hero and Leander,* taken from Ovid's *Heroides* and already made into a highly dramatic scene in his Italian years,[14] and the extremely rare, though not unique scene from the *Aeneid* that Rubens painted about 1630, now in the Johnson Collection in Philadelphia, which was only rather recently identified by Julius Held (Fig. 1)[15]. It shows the immediate cause of the hostilities between the Trojans and the Rutuli, the unfortunate accident that occurred during a hunt in which Aeneas' son Ascanius wounded a tame stag, the favorite animal of Tyrrhus and his daughter Silvia:

> " . . . from bent bow
> Ascanius eager for a hunter's praise,
> Let go his shaft . . .
> . . . whistling through the air,
> The light-winged reed pierced deep in flank and side.

Rubens, Ascanius. Philadelphia, John G. Johnson Collection [Fig. 1]

Swift to its cover fled the wounded thing . . .
Then Silvia the sister smiting oft
On breast and arm, made cry for help and called
The sturdy rustics forth in gathering throng.
These now (for in the silent forest crouched
The cruel Fury) swift to battle flew.
One brandished a charred stake, another swung
A knotted cudgel, as rude anger shapes
Its weapon of whate'er the searching eye
First haps to fall on." (VII, lines 501-508)

In an important letter which Rubens wrote to Franciscus Junius on August 1, 1637, congratulating him on the completion of his book on ancient painting *(De Pictura Veterum),* he speaks of the frustrating impossibility of grasping the greatness of ancient painting from mere descriptions (he compares it with Orpheus' trying to grasp the shade of Euridice) and of those "whom I follow with the greatest veneration and whose footsteps I adore without venturing the claim, even in my own mind, of being able to attain their excellence" (quos ego veneratione summa prosequor, et vestigia euntium potius adoro, quam vel sola cogitatione assequi me posse ingenue profiteor).[16]

Those who ask how Rubens, with his vast activity as a painter, as a highly skilled and successful diplomat (a real power in European politics for many years, not an occasional dabbler as so many people are apt to assume, or are encouraged by popular accounts to believe), as a teacher, as a family man, and indefatigable correspondent, could possibly have found the time to read classical literature are invited to read the report of the Danish physician and traveler, Dr. Otto Sperling, which tried to indicate how that was possible:[17] "We also visited the world-famous painter Rubens, whom we chanced upon while he was working, and at the same time dictating a letter as well as having somebody read from Tacitus to him. We kept quiet so as not to disturb him but he started talking to us while continuing to work, to dictate the letter and to being read to, and also answered our questions . . . After this, he called upon a servant to take us through his magnificent palace and to show us his antiques and his other Greek and Roman statues, of which he owned great quantities." Even if one must suppose that this report follows a conventional pattern, yet essentially it records the way he must have lived.

This visit occurred in 1621. In the same year Rubens received the first letter from a man who more than any other stimulated his interest in the classics, and thus began an exchange of letters touching upon innumerable questions concerning the civilization, beliefs, laws, and artistic endeavors of the ancients. This man was the French scholar Nicolas-Claude Fabri de Peiresc (1580-1637), Counselor of the Parliament of Provence, great traveler, insatiable investigator and collector, and an indefatigable correspondent on all fields of learning and the arts.[18] Rubens and Peiresc met only once, in Paris in 1622, when the painter came to the capital to discuss the plan of his cycle from the life of Marie de' Medici with the queen herself. Soon after, Peiresc moved to Aix-en-Provence but the correspondence flourished from 1622 to about 1630 (many of these letters are lost) and again from 1634 until 1637, the year of Peiresc's death. The scope of this correspondence is amazing, and that the painter-diplomat should have been the peer of the writer-scholar in philological and archaeological matters is a constant source of wonderment.

In August, 1630, Rubens acknowledged receipt from Peiresc of a dissertation with drawings which deals with an ancient tripod that had recently been discovered near Aix-en-Provence. It is characteristic of Rubens and important in our present context that he did not look at this object from the artistic viewpoint only but also from that of an archaeologist and philologist proper. This is how he dwelt upon the meaning of the word tripod: "In the first place, all utensils which rest on three feet were called 'tripods' by the Ancients, even though they served the most varied purposes, such as tables, stools, candelabra, pots, etc. And among other things they had a utensil to set on the fire under the *lebes* (*chaudron* in French) for cooking meat, and this is still used today in many parts of Europe. Then they made a combination of the *lebes* and tripod, much like our iron and bronze pots with three feet. But the Ancients gave it the most beautiful proportions and, in my opinion, this was the true tripod mentioned by Homer and other Greek poets and historians, which was adopted *in re culinaria* for cooking meats. And with regard to the use of entrails in their sacrifices, they began to have [them] *inter sacram supellectilem ad eundem usum.* I do not believe, however, that the Delphic Tripod was of this type, but rather a kind of seat on three legs, as is still commonly used throughout Europe . . . But the point which has more bearing on our subject I shall state with more care, and that is, that the Ancients used a certain kind of chafingdish or *réchaud* (as they say in French) made of bronze, with a double coating in every part, to resist the fire. This was in the form of a tripod, and was used in their sacrifices and perhaps also in their banquets. There is no doubt that this was the tripod of bronze so often mentioned in the Ecclesiastical History of Eusebius, and by other authors—the tripod which served for burning incense to their idols—as you will see in the references below. And if I am not greatly mistaken, this bronze tripod of yours, considering its material, its small size, and the simplicity of workmanship, is one of those which was used to burn incense in the sacrifices. The hole in the middle served as an air-hole to make the coals burn better; just as all modern *réchauds* must still have one or many apertures for this purpose. And as far as one can see from the drawing, the bottom of the basin, or crater, is broken and consumed by the fire. That is all I can say at present on this subject, leaving to you freedom and authority to criticize . . . Everyone marvels that, in so great a public calamity, you remain with mind so composed that you can, with customary pleasure, continue your noble research in the observation *rerum antiquarum. Specimen animi bene compositi et vera philosophia imbuti.*"[19]

In a postscript to this richly illustrated letter, Rubens adds that the passages supporting his view (they are from Pausanias, Isidorus, Julius Pollux, and Surius) "have been added by my son Albert, who is seriously engaged in the study of Antiquities, and is making progress in Greek letters. He honors your name above all . . ." Albert was then sixteen years old!

But it is of course impossible to separate Rubens the philologist and archaeologist (in the narrower sense of the word) from the Rubens who lived primarily by his eyes and to whom every word from antiquity evoked at once an image from antiquity. Emil Kieser has pointed out that his all-encompassing concept of the tripod was to a degree the result of this very fact.[20] This visual relationship to the classical tradition was founded in his eight years in Italy, where he never lost an opportunity to become intimately acquainted with all relics of the ancient past, be they statues, reliefs, paintings, cameos, costumes, weapons, tripods, or anything else; it culminated in his avid collecting of ancient sculpture and of gems and cameos, and the correspondence with Peiresc is again a reliable guide to what ancient works moved Rubens' mind and heart in those later years.

The very first extant letter from Rubens to Peiresc is dated August 3, 1623, and begins with these characteristic sentences: "Monsieur, I have never in my life seen anything that gives me more pleasure than the gems you have sent me. They seem to me inestimable, and beyond all my expectations; but to accept them as a gift, and deprive you of such valuable things is not my intention. Believe me, were it not that I am afraid you will perhaps have departed before the arrival of this letter, I should send them back today by the same courier . . . In the meantime, toward the end of next September I shall send you some good impressions of them."[21] Later in this letter, after a digression on the then extremely popular matter of designs for perpetual motion apparatus, he returns to the gems which were of the ithyphallic sort; he analyzes one of them which he calls *divina vulva*, agrees with Peiresc's interpretation of it as a glorification of female fertility, adds a design of it (in the Leonardesque tradition), and expresses himself in his own Latin on the most delicate features of the object.

Peiresc's admiration for Rubens' knowledge of archaeological details was expressed in an important letter of December 1, 1622, which he wrote to the painter after introducing members of the French court to the *modelli* Rubens had made for tapestries depicting the *History of Constantine* and which the painter had sent to Paris on the recommendation of Peiresc. Here we find the following remark: "They admired your exactness in rendering antique costumes, including even the nails of the boots which I observed with the greatest pleasure on one of the followers of Maxentius." But the same letter also indicates that Peiresc did not find it easy to defend some of the artistic licenses taken by Rubens, even the most justifiable, to that same group of courtiers, and it is quite amusing to watch him squirming at the difficult task of reconciling his admiration for Rubens with his archaeological conscience and his obligation toward his and Rubens' prospective patrons: "The *Allocution* which I liked very much because of the exact rendering of the antique military costumes, found many critics, although only with regard to the way you design the legs in an arc rather than straight according to custom. I remember well that you said to me once (in connection with those fine curved legs of Fréminet's *Moses* and *St. Paul*) that in nature this effect certainly occurs, and the critics cannot deny the truth of nature's effect. But they reply that it is due to a defect or a national characteristic (there are countries where all, or practically all, have deformed legs); and since the ancient sculptors as well as Michelangelo, Raphael, Correggio, Titian have avoided it, it seems that one ought to avoid it still today. Eyes accustomed to their method of representation cannot without a great effort accept such a different approach. Your cartoons would be viewed with enthusiasm by all if it were not for this particularity which is not to the taste of our nation, and if you will listen to the advice of your servant, you will adjust yourself in the future to this infirmity of our eyes. The painters of Ethiopia represent the Madonna with a black face in the Moorish custom; but if Michelangelo or Raphael were to paint today figures with such legs they, too, would be subjected to sharp criticism. And if in the paintings of the [Medici] gallery you do not resolve to use natural postures except where curved legs do appear, you will find little satisfaction. You have to do with some rather obtuse people who are accustomed to something they think quite different. The ancient Egyptians who nearly all had deformed legs gave this same position to their figures and I think they would have considered them deformed without that flaw." And then, the final blow: "Those of our French painters who ignore rules [libertini] do the same."[22] If there was a comment on this by Rubens it has not survived.

But with these characteristic passages of 1622 and 1630 we have run far ahead of the period which was decisive in laying the foundations of the master's comprehensive knowledge of ancient works of art, and I hasten to take you back to his Italian sojourn of 1600 to 1608. Undoubtedly he had seen reproductions of some great works of ancient art before he left Antwerp, but we know little about this, and the few works we can date before 1600 show no clear evidence of it; his pre-Italian copies, all pen drawings, were mostly made after such popular works as sixteenth-century Bible illustrations in woodcut and the like.[23]

Recent research has made it possible for us to distinguish a bit more clearly than before between works executed by Rubens in his early and in his later Italian years. The reflection of antique works of art in those paintings and drawings provides some indication of the time in which he became acquainted with them. Later I shall concentrate on the *way* in which he copied and then transformed those ancient models; here I must restrict myself almost entirely to a catalogue of that group of works, augmented by some notation of Rubens' activity as an avid collector of antique works in his later years and of some of the copies he made for purposes of publication.

The record of his study of classical monuments during his Italian sojourn is confined almost entirely to drawings from *sculpture.* Julius Held, one of the best connoisseurs of Rubens' drawings, has aptly remarked that "a list of the drawings after classical sculpture of which we still have Rubens' originals, augmented by those of which we have copies or which are recorded in old inventories, reads like a roll call of all the celebrated marbles known in his time."[24] Leaving aside the vast number of other antique objects that appealed to his insatiable curiosity, objects pertaining to religious rites, to domestic and musical activities, to military campaigns, and also the few examples known to him of Roman painting such as the *Aldobrandini Wedding,* we find that as early as 1608, at the end of these Italian years, he was thoroughly acquainted with the *Laocoön,* the *Torso Belvedere,* the *Farnese Hercules* and *Bull,* the *Dioscuri,* the *Spinario,* the *Hermaphrodite,* the *African Fisherman* (then thought to represent Seneca), the *Centaur with Cupid on his Back,* the Column of Trajan, the Arch of Titus, and many other works of this kind, not to mention a large group of portrait busts, sarcophagus reliefs, gems, cameos and coins. As you can see, this is all late Hellenistic and Roman work; we cannot tell whether he distinguished between Roman copies of Greek works and Roman sculpture proper but we can be sure that he knew little or nothing of classical Greek art except by way of Roman copies, even later in his life. To the items listed here others can be added if we assume, as seems to be reasonable, that the so-called *Copenhagen Sketch Book* which contains a large number of copies after drawings by Rubens plus a few originals was at least partly based on early copies after the antique by Rubens himself.[25]

To this vast store already accumulated by the year 1608 Rubens added treasure after treasure during the following Antwerp years—the years when he built himself a large house and when the craving to become a collector on a large scale became irresistible. The climax came in 1618. On March 17 and April 28 of that year, Rubens wrote the two famous letters[26] to Sir Dudley Carleton, who had then just been appointed British ambassador to the Hague (situated in what was officially enemy territory for the Southern Netherlander Rubens, although this was the time of the precarious Twelve Years' Truce between the two countries). In these letters he proposed the exchange of a number of his own paintings for Carleton's collection of ancient works; and to the second of them we owe the invaluable list in which the master described with the greatest care the exact degree of authenticity with regard to each painting. The bargain was concluded on May 20, 1618, and was confirmed by Rubens with a sigh of relief in Latin: "Quod utrique nostrum felix faustumque sit!" (May it be a happy and blessed occasion for both of us!)[27]

Carleton chose six pictures which Rubens had specifically designated as having been painted entirely by his own hand and which were valued at 3000 guilders, plus 1000 guilders worth of other pictures and 2000 in cash. Rubens received 21 large statues, 8 statues of children, 4 torsos, 57 heads, 17 pedestals, 5 urns, 4 bas-reliefs, 18 busts of Roman emperors, plus sundry fragments and small pieces.[28] Of these works very little is known. None of the many Flemish painters of artists' studios has left us a reliable representation of the interior of Rubens' house. The group of ancient statues and busts which one sees in the background of a fanciful *Rubens' Studio* by Cornelius de Baellieur in the Pitti Palace in Florence can give us only a very general idea of the original.[29] The Carleton marbles remained in Rubens' possession until 1627, when most of them made part of the collection he sold to the Duke of Buckingham, supplemented by a large group of medals and gems, and paintings by himself and by other masters; for this Buckingham paid Rubens 100,000 guilders.[30] About the same time, Rubens sold to Daniel Fourment another group of antique objects which included the so-called *Rubens Vase,* a beautiful large agate vase with vine leaf carvings of the fourth or fifth century A.D., which he had bought in Paris for 2000 gold scudi and which after fantastic peregrinations has now found a permanent home in the Walters Art Gallery in Baltimore (Fig. 2).[31]

These transactions mark the end of a vast collecting effort on

The Rubens Vase. Baltimore, Walters Art Gallery [Fig. 2]

the part of Rubens but not of his profound interest in all facets of ancient civilization and art. The reopened correspondence with Peiresc, 1634-1637, shows him as enthusiastic about the entire field as ever, including ancient painting; the *Aldobrandini Wedding,* which had been discovered in Rome when Rubens was in Italy (1606), had already been described by him, "memoriter et ex tempore," but with considerable accuracy, in a letter to Peiresc, dated May 19, 1628,[32] in which he asked the French scholar for a colored drawing of it. I shall take up here the story of some actual copies by Rubens which are distinguished from the examples discussed later in this book by the fact that they were meant to be *objective documents* concerning ancient works, made, not for the artist's private use but for other scholars.

Such copies by Rubens are relatively rare, and they were made with the more or less certain intention of being used in learned treatises. The *pièces de résistance* in this category are his copies of the two great cameos which he and Peiresc planned to publish in a book, together with other works of this kind.

Gemma Tiberiana. Paris, Bibliothèque Nationale

[Fig. 3]

Rubens, Gemma Tiberiana. Antwerp, Museum Plantin-Moretus

[Fig. 4]

These drawings are slightly larger than the originals. The so-called *Gemma Tiberiana,* which represents the *Glorification of Germanicus* (Fig. 3), had been discovered by Peiresc in the Treasury of the Sainte Chapelle in 1620. It was copied by Rubens with fidelity when he visited Paris in 1622 in connection with the commission for the Marie de' Medici Cycle, which will claim our attention later. The drawing is now in the Plantin–Moretus Museum in Antwerp (Fig. 4).[33] The effect of the contrast between the white and the colored layers in the sardonyx is perhaps somewhat underplayed. The engraving after this drawing was sent by Rubens to Valavez, Peiresc's brother, on July 3, 1625.[34] But there is more. When Rubens left Paris after his second visit, in June, 1623, he promised Peiresc to make a colored drawing of the same cameo, as a companion piece to one of the *Gemma Augustea,* painted by Niccolò dell'Abbate and already owned by Peiresc.[35] Instead, he painted a copy of it *en grisaille* on canvas, three times the original size,[36] which Peiresc received with the greatest joy and enthusiasm on June 19, 1626 (Fig. 5).[37]

Rubens, Gemma Tiberiana. Polesden Lacey, C. Norris Collection [Fig. 5]

As to its relationship to the original, we are fortunate enough to have Rubens' own words in his letter to Valavez of April 2, 1626: "In order to avoid the most serious difficulties it has been necessary to give up the attempt to observe so precisely all the variations in the stone which you probably remember, as, for example, the white, which becomes more pallid or gray in places. I have been obliged to represent only the white and the upper and under layers of the sardonyx. I hope that the Councilor, your brother, great connoisseur that he is, will find some satisfaction in it."[38] Rubens thus corrected what he may have considered a fault in his own earlier drawing.

The *Gemma Augustea* (Fig. 6) had already been copied by Rubens before October 27, 1621, when Peiresc referred to such a drawing and asked to borrow it for a comparison with the newly discovered *Tiberiana*.[39] The history of the *Gemma Augustea* is still somewhat obscure, and I do not know whether—and if so, when and where—Rubens saw the original; stolen from the

[Fig. 6] Gemma Augustea. Vienna, Kunsthistorisches Museum

Cabinet du Roy in 1591, it seems to have been in Emperor Rudolf's possession by the late 1590's, but casts may have circulated even before that time, and, as just mentioned, it had already been painted on a large scale by Niccolò dell'Abbate. In any case, Rubens seems to have known it for some time before 1621, as I shall try to show later. The drawing now in the Lübeck Museum (Fig. 7)[40] is most probably the one he made at Paris in 1623 from the sulphur cast in Peiresc's possession which is mentioned in Peiresc's letter to Jacob Cools dated June 27, 1623.[41] A comparison of this drawing with the cameo clearly indicates that Rubens was here less concerned with the specific coloristic effects than he was in the drawing, let alone the painting, of the *Tiberiana.* He probably had less time for it, but the wonderful spontaneity with which all the main features were jotted down with chalk, pen, and bister wash makes this an artistically superior achievement and does convey much of the glow of the original, even though in a general rather than specific

Rubens, Gemma Augustea. Lübeck, Museum. [Fig. 7]

way. The engraving after the drawing was sent to Valavez together with that of the *Tiberiana* in 1625.[42] The planned publication never materialized.

Other than these, relatively few strictly documentary drawings by Rubens after ancient works of art exist. Four were made for, or in any event used in, his brother's book which appeared under the title *Electorum Libri Duo* in Antwerp in 1608;[43] a series of copies from classical heads, mostly portrait busts, may have been destined for a publication that came to naught,[44] and I shall return to some of them later; drawings after antique coins, such as the series in London and Chatsworth,[45] may have been intended for a similar purpose.

There is additional proof that even in his later years Rubens' enthusiasm was sometimes aroused not by works of ancient art alone but by documents appealing primarily to historians and philologists—and apparently appealing to Rubens for very personal reasons.

On August 8, 1629, he wrote to Pierre Dupuy from London where he was concluding his highly successful peace mission involving England and Spain. In this letter[46] he mentioned in rather general terms of admiration the collection of ancient marbles owned by the Earl of Arundel, perhaps the finest ever assembled in England. But here the philologist-archaeologist Rubens, *and* Rubens the *man,* spoke again as he added: "I confess that I have never seen anything in the world more rare, from the point of view of antiquity, quam foedus ictum inter Smyrnenses et Magnesios cum duobus earundem civitatum decretis et victoriis Publii Citharoedi"—an ancient inscription concerning a treaty between the people of Smyrna and of Magnesia, with the decrees of these two cities and the list of the victories of Publius Citharoedus! It is a touching thing to see this great artist and radiant favorite of the gods rejoice in a bit of history he read from a simple marble inscription because its report on a successful peace treaty, comparable to the one he had just brought into being himself, warmed his heart.

II. Adaptation

The report I have given on Rubens' copies of the two great cameos has anticipated the theme of what I now wish to discuss but differs from it in that those copies were made primarily for purposes of documentation. I shall now turn to copies which he made primarily for his own use: first, to the exact copies or those with comparatively minor changes which he made after ancient works of art, and then, to those in which he leaned heavily on works with classical subjects by other artists.

It will surprise no one that these examples belong chiefly to the master's formative years, that is, to his sojourn in Italy from 1600 to 1608 and to the earlier phase of his Antwerp period, from about 1609 to 1615. However, in his later years Rubens did not cease to copy works of art that appealed to him; a spectacular case in point occurred during his stay in Madrid in 1628, when the overwhelming impact of the art of the late Titian caused him to copy many of his works. On the other hand it is true that in later life this copying was a strictly private matter, even when he made painted copies, whereas in his earlier years he had often not hesitated to incorporate his copies or near copies (all drawings) in works for which he was commissioned or which were in any case destined for sale—a procedure which was of course quite common and fully sanctioned in a happy world of art that had not yet been infected with the originality virus.

As we turn to Rubens' study material from the vast field of ancient statues and reliefs we are faced with a veritable *embarras de richesse.*[1] Although we have to do exclusively with drawings, the mere technical diversity is astonishing. Rubens used pen and ink in some cases, various types of chalk in others—black, red, and white chalk, sometimes washed with bister and heightened with body color, sometimes with added water color or gouache. While straight pen and ink was normally used for rapid sketches, a custom continued by Rubens into his late years, studies properly speaking were either restricted to or based upon chalk or several chalks. But within this medium he invariably produced that blend of accuracy and revitalization which was the hallmark of all his efforts in this field.

His virtuosity can be appreciated through a comparison of almost any of his copies with those made after the same model by older Netherlandish masters such as Jan Gossaert, Martin van Heemskerck, or Frans Floris; only a few of Hendrick Goltzius' finest efforts approach those of Rubens.[2]

The *Laocoön* (Fig. 8), discovered in 1506, had played a decisive role in the days of Michelangelo and for a long time continued to be one of the most celebrated ancient marbles. We have now, after a very recent discovery of a large group of Rubens' drawings in the Ambrosiana in Milan,[3] no less than

[Fig. 8] Laocoön. Rome, Vatican

six copies of it by Rubens himself, and school drawings which have preserved what look like several other views and details sketched by the master in Italy. The drawing of the whole group in the Ambrosiana[4] gives the main frontal view in black and some white chalk (Fig. 9). The Dresden drawing in black chalk[5] is of the father-priest, three-quarter length, facing to the right, viewed from nearby and from an extremely low view point. The Ambrosiana find has also yielded a back view of the father, a frontal view of the elder son alone, and two of the younger son alone, one from the front and the other from the back.[6] All were apparently made from the original in the Roman years 1606-1608.

The number of transformations of these motifs in works by Rubens is considerable, and I shall return to some of them later; however, the figure of Laocoön was once used in a context which did not require significant changes of either content or form. There is one biblical story that involves people over-

Rubens, Laocoön. Milan, Ambrosiana [Fig. 9]

powered by serpents, namely that of the "Erection of the Brazen Serpent" by Moses; and the degree to which, more than thirty years later, Rubens was still under the influence of forms studied so assiduously in his early years can be gauged by looking at the man in armor on the right of the London painting of about 1638 (Fig. 10):[7] he is Laocoön in reverse. The appearance of the motif in a mirror image would suggest, in the case of any minor artist, the use of an engraving made after the original; the direct and complete sovereignty over material of this kind is a prerogative of a great master. That Rubens was capable of performing such feats without mechanical help of any kind almost stands to reason. But we should not forget that he never neglected to study a statue from every angle, thus intensifying his knowledge of its inner coherence and the relationship of its parts far beyond simple frontal and lateral views, even where those more complicated views were unimportant to their creator. A famous example of this kind is Rubens' representation of

[Fig. 10] Rubens, Erection of the Brazen Serpent. London, National Gallery

Michelangelo's *Notte* from the back, a view which of course the Florentine master never intended to be seen.[8]

The Torso Belvedere (Fig. 11), the signed work of Apollonius, son of Nestor, was probably studied by Rubens from the original in the Belvedere, for which it had been acquired by Clement VII; no bronze or plaster versions of the marble seem to have existed at that time. The thoroughness of Rubens' studies is attested by the copy in black chalk, now in the Rubenshuis in Antwerp (Fig. 12),[9] and by two pen sketches in Copenhagen which have just been claimed as the master's own rather than a pupil's, as was hitherto assumed;[10] the latter two show the statue from the back. The Antwerp study renders Apollonius' work with the greatest fidelity, including the inscription and all the details of damage and imperfection. Even in this very early copy, however, subtle reinforcements of outer and inner contour lines, together with an increase in undulation and the interrelating of all parts achieved through this device, has imparted a

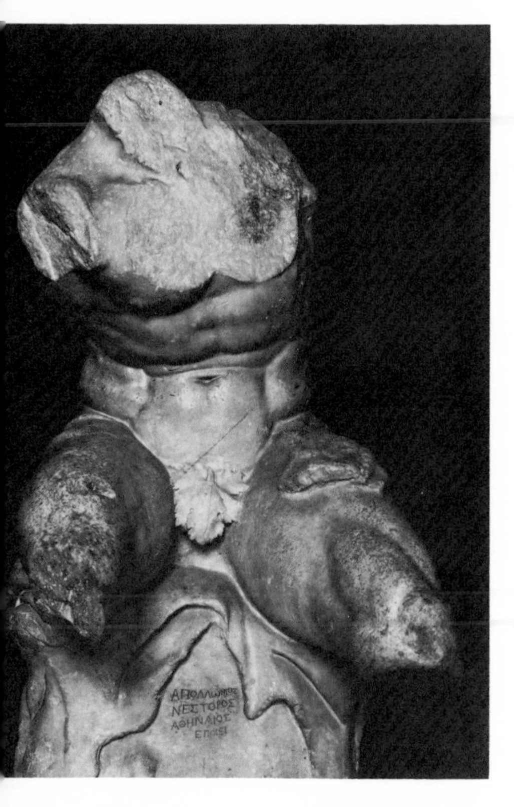

11] Torso Belvedere. Rome, Vatican

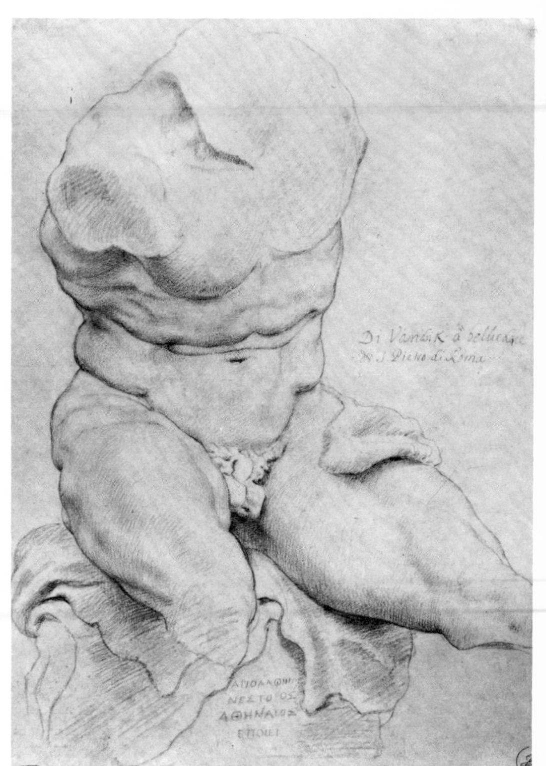

Rubens, Torso Belvedere. Antwerp, Rubenshuis [Fig. 12]

liveliness, an energy, a dynamic power to the image which the original only suggests and which are found with comparable vigor in copies of the *Torso* by only one other master: those made in 1591 by Hendrick Goltzius, one of Holland's greatest draftsmen.[11] If we did not know that such copies were copies at all, we should probably think of them as typical works of Rubens' time in general and of Rubens in particular, just as this is true of some other great masters who became "creative copyists"—Dürer, Delacroix, Cézanne come readily to mind.

It is in this connection that Rubens' own words on a sound and profitable study of ancient sculpture can be quoted in full support of what he has placed before our eyes in his drawings and paintings. Rubens wrote, we do not exactly know when, a very eloquent Latin treatise with the title *De imitatione statuarum,* the only finished or, in any case, the only surviving section of a much larger body of writings he seems to have contemplated.[12] It has been somewhat neglected by recent writers and is not even readily available in English translation. For us, its most important sentences are the following: [The imitation of ancient statues is] "for some most useful, for others detrimental to the extent of the very annihilation of their art (*aliis utilissima, aliis damnosa usque ad exterminium artis*). I am convinced that in order to achieve the highest perfection [in that art] one needs a full understanding of the statues, nay a complete absorption in them; but one must make judicious use of them and before all avoid the effect of stone. For many neophytes and even some experts do not distinguish stuff from form, stone from figure, nor the exigencies of the marble from its artistic use . . . Whoever can make this distinction with wise discretion should indeed welcome the statues in a loving embrace; for what can we, decadent children of this erring century, accomplish? What vile spirit keeps us weaklings fettered to the ground, far away from that heroic stature and natural insight? We may still be afflicted by the darkness in which our forefathers lived; maybe the Gods have suffered us to fall from past errors into worse ones, or, to our irreparable loss, to be weakened by a decaying world; perhaps it is also true that in former centuries the human body, closer to the origin and perfection of things, was granted freely that strength which now, through the fault of decadent ages and of corrupting influences, has come to naught, abandoning its perfection to the growing vices; it is proved by the testimony of many that the stature of man has gradually diminished, as secular and sacred sources of the age of heroes, giants, and cyclopes have told us in many fabulous but also some indubitably correct reports . . ."

It is a sad reflection of what Dürer called the "blindness of judgment that dwells within us" that even Roger de Piles, the fortunate owner of this treatise by Rubens and an enlightened champion of the master in many respects, should have written in 1699: "Tho' Rubens lived seven years in Italy; tho' he made a considerable collection of medals, statues, and engraved stones; tho' he examined, understood and extolled the beauty of the Antique, as appears by a ms. of his, the original of which is in my custody, yet, thro' education, and the nature of his country, he fell into a Flemish character, and sometimes made an ill choice, offending against the regularity of design: However, tho' this is a fault that is blameable wherever it is found, and tho' his knitting of the joints is a little too extravagant, yet the best judges must confess that Rubens was very far from being ignorant in designing . . . "[13] Like Peiresc, de Piles *had* to defend the cause of straight legs *versus* "knitted" joints; after all, they were both French.

Returning to other classical models, two highly admired antique marbles thoroughly studied by Rubens during his Roman journeys have remained connected with the name of the Farnese Family: The Farnese Bull and the Hercules Farnese. The huge group of the Bull, today in the National Museum in Naples, was found in 1456 in the Baths of Caracalla; it had been described by Pliny as the work of Apollonius (certainly not identical with the master of the Torso) and Tauriskos of Tralles. Rubens was not concerned with the complicated story about Dirke who is bound to the bull by Amphion and Zetos in order to suffer the same gruesome fate she had planned for the twin brothers. In his black chalk drawing,[14] he concentrated on the bull alone as seen from below, emphasizing its muscular contours. A red chalk drawing of the Hercules Farnese is perhaps a very early drawing by Rubens;[15] a later one (of 1606/08) has recently been found in the Ambrosiana.[16] A brilliant chalk drawing in Moscow (Fig. 13)[17] preserves Rubens' faithful rendering of one of the many existing Roman copies of a lost Hellenistic bronze of a centaur being teased by an impudent cupid riding on his back; Rubens used it later for the *Education of Achilles,* in which Chiron is the master.[18] And a Silenus, now in the Dresden Sculpture Collection but then in the possession of Agostino Chigi in Rome, has been identified as the model of a splendid Rubens drawing in the British Museum.[19]

A fascinating chapter in the history of misinterpretation and adaptation of the subject and form of an ancient statue is the one pertaining to the so-called *Seneca.* This statue, now considered to be of an African fisherman, has survived in several versions; Rubens knew the one then in the Villa Borghese, later

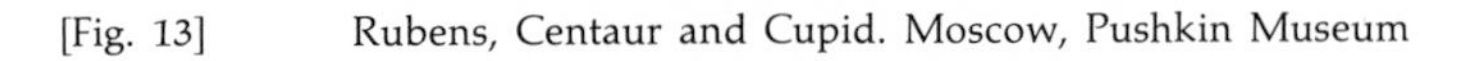

[Fig. 13] Rubens, Centaur and Cupid. Moscow, Pushkin Museum

acquired by the Louvre (Fig. 14). In his time, it was believed to represent the Stoic philosopher, dramatist, and statesman Seneca, whom Nero, as Tacitus reports, forced to commit suicide by bleeding to death in his bath. The version in the Vatican, showing the feet, refutes this interpretation, which the Borghese statue, cut above the feet, had encouraged.

When Rubens copied the statue (I am illustrating one of the three drawings preserved in the Hermitage in Leningrad, Fig. 15)[20] he did so faithfully, with two exceptions. First, at the bottom he added the bathtub required by the current interpretation; second, he gave to the head of the man a spiritual character altogether missing from the features of the original. This character was not added arbitrarily but had its origin in an antique bust which Rubens knew in detail and even owned, an excellent piece of Roman art, which has likewise survived in several versions and which was considered a portrait of Seneca by some (it is now believed to be an "invented" Hellenistic portrait of

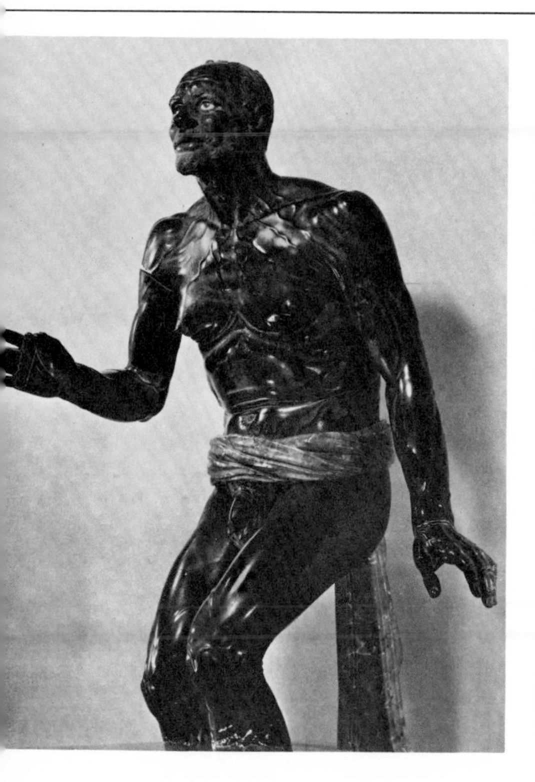

14] African Fisherman. Paris, Louvre

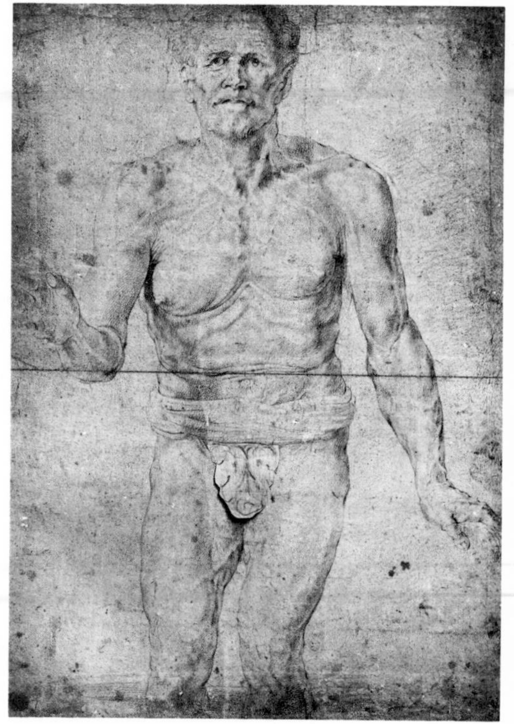

Rubens, "Seneca." Leningrad, Hermitage [Fig. 15]

Hesiod).[21] This head was carefully and beautifully drawn, mostly with pen and ink, on a sheet at present in the Robert Lehman Collection in New York.[22] There exist also two painted versions by Rubens.[23] It was about 1612-1615 that Rubens painted the magnificent group portrait now in the Pitti Palace in Florence (Fig. 16), which shows the artist himself, his brother Philip the philologist, their learned friend Jan de Wouwere, and the great philologist Justus Lipsius assembled before a Roman landscape and under that same bust of Seneca; later Rubens placed the bust above the entrance to his studio (Fig. 66). The painting was probably done in loving memory not only of Lipsius, who had died in 1606, but also of Philip Rubens, who died in 1611.

At about this same time Rubens painted the *Dying Seneca* in Munich (Fig. 17).[24] The early drawing was brilliantly incorporated into the narrative of the philosopher's last moments, with a young man reverently writing down the words of the dying

[Fig. 16] Rubens, Justus Lipsius and Disciples. Florence, Palazzo Pitti

man, whose features have gained significantly in spiritual power even in comparison with that drawing. Rubens' intensive preoccupation with this ancient author is easy to understand; his stoic philosophy appealed to him, and his death was that of a great hero. He was also a man who, more than any other victim of imperial persecution, was considered a prototype of Christian martyrdom and correspondingly revered by Rubens' fellow Catholics. In the Munich picture this admission of the pagan philosopher to the ranks of Christian martyrs was sanctioned, as it were, by the fact that he was made the center of a group containing representatives of authority, discipleship, and pity, in the finest tradition of Christian altarpieces. A magnificent side view of the Fisherman–Seneca has been discovered in the Ambrosiana;[25] a three-quarter view is in Leningrad.[26]

Next to antique statues, and in addition to the cameos and coins discussed earlier, other monuments of ancient art attracted

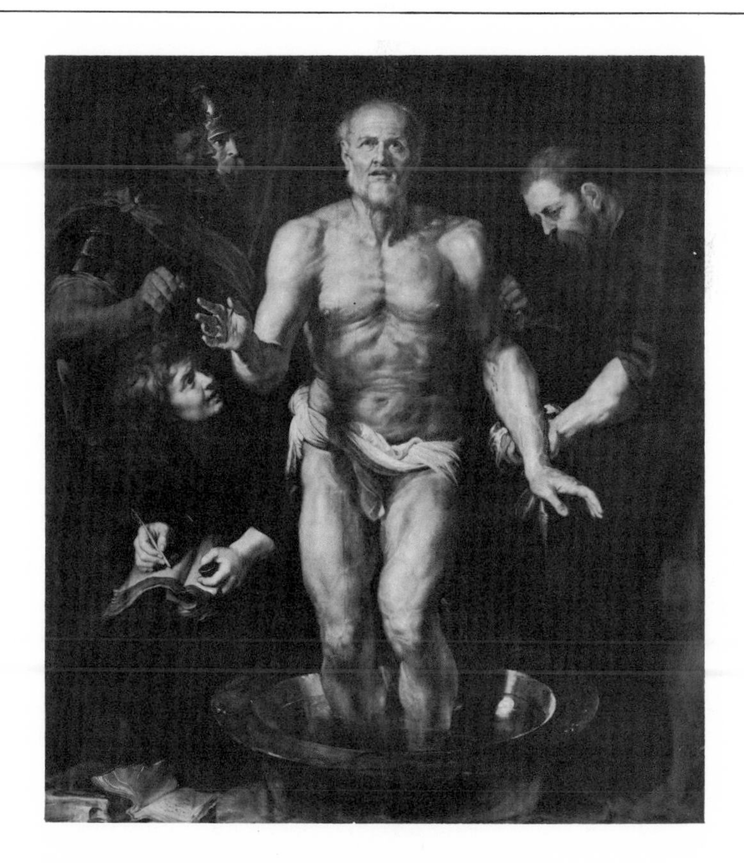

Rubens, Dying Seneca. Munich, Alte Pinakothek [Fig. 17]

Rubens' insatiable curiosity: a number of reliefs from sarcophagi and from the columns and arches of Rome, and portrait busts. A few words on these two groups must suffice.

During a visit to the Villa Mattei in his early Roman years, Rubens chanced upon a fine sarcophagus (Fig. 18), the right end of which represented a poet standing between two Muses, and he was fascinated by it. On a sheet now in the Art Institute of Chicago (Fig. 19),[27] he first jotted down in black chalk the three figures, then turned his special attention to the center figure and repeated its head in larger size to the left. Finally with the pen he added two inscriptions. Next to the center character we find the words "Socrates procul dubio" (Socrates, without doubt), and next to the right Muse "Xantippe qua stomachatur" (Xantippe by whom he is vexed) and "vide os columnatum" (look at that face supported upon the hand). As Julius Held has pointed out the latter phrase is a quotation from Plautus, with whose

[Fig. 18] Sarcophagus, detail. Rome, Terme

work Rubens was well acquainted; it occurs in the *Miles Gloriosus* (lines 210-212), where the attitude of a man hatching a clever plan is characterized as "support of the chin with a pillar" and another Roman poet is reported to have an "os columnatum"—a unique expression invented by Plautus to fit this particular comparison. I believe that Professor Held was entirely justified in thinking of these inscriptions as a learned joke, probably addressed to, or aimed at, his brother Philip, who is known to have been fond of quoting Plautus. That Rubens should have mistaken the right Muse for Xantippe is even less probable than that he should have mistaken the male figure for Socrates. It is also to be noted that he worked out the two right figures in greater detail than the left Muse, thus suggesting a special emphasis upon, and a fictitious conversation between, the two, and that he gave to the perfectly innocuous-looking Muse of the original a vulgar expression which makes the "os

Rubens, copy from sarcophagus. Chicago, Art Institute of Chicago [Fig. 19]

columnatum" quotation sound very appropriate. Archaeology, philology, high artistry, and a subtle sense of humor—what an extraordinary combination! As extraordinary as the combination of painting, dictating, being read to, and entertaining visitors all at the same time, which Dr. Sperling so vividly depicted.

Another instance of very close copying from an ancient relief is the *Drunken Hercules* of about 1613 in Dresden (Fig. 20). Emil Kieser, to whom we owe one of the most lucid articles on Rubens,[28] more than thirty years ago showed that Rubens used a Roman relief in circular form which we know only from an engraving of 1779 after an original in the Mattei Collection in Rome (Fig. 21) and which in turn is closely related to a sarcophagus in Athens. Nobody will overlook the magnificent small adjustments through which Rubens went beyond the ancient model, and particularly the skillful transformation of the round into the near-square format, which suggested the addition of

[Fig. 20] Rubens, Drunken Hercules. Dresden Museum

the splendid side figures. Nevertheless, this is a case of an unusually direct adaptation of the classical work in a finished painting.

As has already been intimated, several of Rubens' drawings of portrait busts may have been made with the intention of publishing them in a corpus of the kind planned for the cameos and the coins and likewise doomed to failure. We have some wonderful specimens of this sort which betray an extraordinary insight into the character of the portrayed, either translated faithfully from the original or reinforced and perhaps even newly introduced in Rubens' copy. The magnificent drawing of Julius Caesar in the Louvre[29] was made as preparation for an engraving by the excellent print-maker Boetius a Bolswert; its execution is highly sophisticated technically, using as it does black chalk, pen strokes, and washes in rust-brown and greenish brown. Others are drawn with the pen alone, perhaps as a *first* step

Drunken Hercules, engraving after Roman relief [Fig. 21]

toward interpretation by the engraver. This is true of the so-called *Seneca,* to which I have referred, as well as of the *Nero* of the Fogg Art Museum (Fig. 22),[30] which was later engraved by Paulus Pontius. This late drawing is based on the bearded bust now in the Capitoline Museum.[31]

I should mention the few instances in which Rubens' copies after ancient works of art have preserved pieces which we should otherwise not know, either in their entirety or at least in their unrestored state. One example from each category will have to suffice. The originals of a black chalk drawing by Rubens (Fig. 23), one of the group rediscovered in the Ambrosiana,[32] have not yet been identified and seem to have disappeared. The river god in the upper center of the drawing is of minor interest; but the figure drawn from two slightly different angles on the right and left must have been a piece of considerable importance. The subject, not unusual in ancient art, is undoubt-

[Fig. 22] Rubens, Nero. Cambridge, Mass., Fogg Art Museum

edly the *Drunken Hercules;* he reclines on his lion's skin, a companion supports his right wrist and pats his right shoulder, and a faun grins at us from behind his left arm. Reminiscences of the figure appear in later paintings by Rubens. One hopes that the search for the lost original has already begun among archaeologists. The group also had some influence on Michelangelo and Raphael and, through the latter's *Judgment of Paris,* on Manet's *Déjeuner sur l'herbe* as well.

The case in which Rubens transmitted most vividly the sad state of preservation of a piece of ancient sculpture known to most of us only in a highly restored condition is that of the Roman *Lupa* with Romulus and Remus—not the famous bronze group but the one tucked away below the huge *Tiber* now in the Louvre, which was found on New Year's Day, 1512, and immediately taken to the Belvedere of the Vatican. From Rubens' chalk copy in the Ambrosiana (Fig. 24)[33] we can now gather

Rubens, copies after the antique. Milan, Ambrosiana [Fig. 23]

that the group was in a rather poor state at that time (a drawing by Goltzius[34] shows this much less clearly). The ears and snout of the wolf were gone, and the children were without heads; both had lost an arm; one, a leg and a foot. Yet, the drawing, in which no change appears except the substitution of reeds for the river god as background, endows the group in its mutilated state with a certain magnificence quite absent in the restored original which we see today. When Rubens adapted this drawing, made on the spot in Rome about 1606-1608, for a painting of his own[35] after his return to Antwerp (Fig. 25), he introduced one very interesting change. This change is all the more fascinating in that it is based on Rubens' careful reading of Vergil's text in the *Aeneid* (VIII, lines 630–634); more, this text, describing the decoration of the shield of Aeneas as wrought by Vulcan, was written by Rubens himself below the drawing: "He had finished, too, the she-wolf outstretched in the green cave of Mars; around her teats the two boys hung playing, and mouthed

[Fig. 24] Rubens, Lupa with Romulus and Remus. Milan, Ambrosiana

their foster-mother without fear; she with sleek neck bent back, licked them by turns and shaped their bodies with her tongue." The licking of the twins was neglected by the artist of the marble; Rubens restored the poet's vision and furthermore gave his painting not only more life through emphasis on the brilliant contrast between the furry texture of the mother and the shining nudity of the children but also a vastly superior compositional order.

A few words are in order concerning the representations of ancient subjects in the copies Rubens made after works by later artists. I shall be very brief about the few works of this kind made in Italy. Among his many copies after Michelangelo are few with classical subjects; only the two known drawings after the *Battle of Centaurs and Lapiths*[36] were made in Italy, and Rubens' main interest here was centered on the problem of lighting the relief; he recorded the light coming from the right in one, from the left in the other drawing. A curious and rather excep-

Rubens, Story of Romulus and Remus. Rome, Museo Capitolino [Fig. 25]

tional case is Rubens' copy after Montorsoli's *Resting Pan,* now in the St. Louis City Art Gallery, which was long considered a free copy of the *Barberini Faun* in Munich (and is of course dependent on the latter).[37] The copies made by Rubens after Leonardo, Raphael,[38] Correggio, Pordenone, and Titian during his Italian sojourn pertain, with some exceptions, to recent history and the Bible. There are some subjects from antiquity among his copies after masters of the Mannerist period such as Polidoro da Caravaggio, Giulio Romano, Perino del Vaga, and Primaticcio, and after contemporaries such as Annibale Carracci; but these studies are of less importance to our subject.

Recently, increased attention has been paid to drawings by these and other masters acquired by Rubens and in many cases retouched by him, either in order to restore them if damaged, or for the sake of making them more his own;[39] they contain some ancient subjects such as the *Story of Phaeton* (by Pirro Ligorio), the *Judgment of Seleucus* (after Giulio Romano), *Heracles pursuing Nessus and Deianira* (by Battista Franco), and *Cupid and Psyche* (after Perino del Vaga). More important to us is the picture which Rubens sold to Sir Dudley Carleton in 1618 as "A Prometheus bound on Mt. Caucasus, with an eagle which pecks his liver. Original by my hand, and the eagle done by Snyders," and which is now in the Philadelphia Museum (Fig. 26).[40] This painting was completed by 1612, thus three years after Rubens' return from Italy, but is undoubtedly a very close adaptation of a famous drawing by Michelangelo, now in Windsor, representing Tityus, who had violated Latona and was punished in Hades by having his liver pecked by vultures—a story closely resembling that of Prometheus. In a chalk drawing, now in the Louvre, Rubens had transformed the Prometheus subject into a *Death of Hippolytus* (who was killed when his horses, frightened by a monster sent by Neptune, bolted); but whereas the oil sketch with *Hippolytus* in Count Seilern's collection is again closer to the Michelangelo model, the *Prometheus* in Philadelphia, preceded by the Louvre drawing, introduces an important change in the position of the legs. In spite of this deviation, the composition of the Philadelphia picture, which Charles Dempsey has shown to be a brilliant "reconstruction" of a painting by Euanthes described by Achilles Tatius,[41] is more obviously of a derivative nature than most other works of the Antwerp period and may therefore find its logical place in this context.

As mentioned before, outright copies became very rare in Rubens' later years, with two exceptions: copies made on commission or for reasons not primarily connected with Rubens' artistic interests, and copies made under the impact of the most decisive artistic experience he had during his visit to Spain in 1628—the realization of the overwhelming greatness of the art of the late Titian. This also explains why these late copies by the master are all *paintings,* not drawings. Titian had meant comparatively little to the draftsman of the Italian years, 1600–1608; now his art became a revelation to the painter whose own artistic development, particularly after about 1620, had tended

Rubens, Prometheus. Philadelphia, Philadelphia Museum of Art [Fig. 26]

in the direction of greater coloristic splendor and refinement. Also, it is hardly surprising to discover that it was Titian as a painter of classical subjects who exerted such a decisive influence on Rubens at that time. His greatest mythological paintings, mostly of his late period but also some earlier ones, had found their way into the royal collections in Madrid, and it is Titian's nudes—in addition to his landscapes, which also deeply affected Rubens—that incorporated most fully and most splendidly his discoveries in the realms of light and texture. Rubens copied a number of such works in Madrid, including the *Rape of Europa,* perhaps the greatest late Titian now in this country (Gardner Museum, Boston, Fig. 27); it is a case of study-copy *pur sang,* and one of exceptional congeniality (Fig. 28).[42]

In addition, I should like to mention Rubens' copy (Fig. 30) of an earlier work by Titian, the *Andrians* (Fig. 29), which formed the companion piece of the *Worship of Venus,* likewise copied by him.[43] These two paintings by Titian had been executed about

[Fig. 27] Titian, Europa. Boston, Isabella Stewart Gardner Museum

1520 for the *Camerino* of Alfons I d'Este in Ferrara, were later in several Roman collections, and did not enter the royal collections in Spain until 1638; consequently, they were not actually seen by Rubens at the time of his visit to Madrid, and perhaps never. All the more astonishing is his achievement, which, as indicated by some slight deviations from the original, seems to have been based on a copy of Titian's original, possibly by van Dyck. Rubens never disposed of the copies after Titian which he made in his late years; they appear in the inventory taken after his death and were only then purchased by Philip IV of Spain; the *Andrians* and the *Worship of Venus* later went via Marshal Bernadotte to the Stockholm Museum. I have not seen them, but good reproductions indicate quite clearly that Rubens translated the originals from the idiom of the *early* Titian into one more closely related to that of the *late* Titian, whose works he so deeply admired and so thoroughly assimilated in 1628. This is not the place for a detailed stylistic com-

Rubens, Europa. Madrid, Prado [Fig. 28]

parison (the less so as John Walker has written an excellent chapter on it).[44] It may be worth stressing again, however, that the change is not so much one from Italian to Flemish art—as the classicist Mengs sadly remarked—as from early Titian to late Rubens, a transformation possible only because of the Flemish master's sympathetic understanding of the late Titian. And if anywhere, it is in the late Titian that Rubens' magnificent revitalization of the classical past had found a congenial predecessor. It is clear that when Rubens made that discovery in Spain his chief reaction was a great eagerness to learn to speak this pictorial language more fluently than he had spoken it before. Pacheco, the father-in-law of Velazquez whom Rubens met during that visit, has told us that the Flemish master, in spite of his heavy diplomatic schedule, managed to copy "all the Titians" in the king's collections.[45] We have no reason to consider this statement an affable hyperbole; rather, it should remind us that a great master never ceases to be a humble and industrious pupil.

[Fig. 29] Titian, The Andrians. Madrid, Prado

Rubens, The Andrians. Stockholm, National Museum [Fig. 30]

III. Transformation

Thus far we have been tracing the roads which Rubens followed as he explored the classical tradition, the literary as well as the visual branch of it, and we have established its approximate content. Beyond that, we have given some indications that this visual heritage was not only studied with greatest care but also that it immediately released in him forces which had lain slumbering in his own not yet fully mature mind. It is this less reproductive, this more truly creative reinterpretation of the inherited forms that will occupy us now.

As early as his first Italian years this propensity for creative reinterpretation is noticeable in the paintings commissioned to him; and any comparison between his pre-Italian works and those painted from 1601 to 1603 will readily show the enormous advance brought about by the impact of his study of ancient art. An extraordinary example of the avalanche of new ideas and forms precipitated by that study has been rediscovered in the Prague Castle Gallery (Fig. 62); but since this is at the same time a composition which represents what seems to be a contemporary event in the guise of mythology I shall postpone describing it until later.

I here revert to Rubens' use of ancient forms for biblical characters, which we observed in the adaptation of the *Laocoön* for one of the victims of the serpent from the Old Testament. The representation of pagan and biblical personages on equal terms by virtue of their physical and moral sufferings or beauty, is of course known to us from the masters of the High Renaissance proper, particularly from Raphael and the early Michelangelo. But it is important to realize that this happy symbiosis had deteriorated under the heavy hand of the Counter-Reformation—speaking art-historically, during the period of Mannerism—

and that it was the early Baroque masters, and Rubens in particular, who restored that happy equilibrium and gave it new and powerful expression—another important point in favor of Jacob Burckhardt's rapprochement between Renaissance and Baroque. Rubens' *Saint Sebastian* (Fig. 31) and his *Andromeda* (Fig. 32),[1] while embodying two different phases of his career, will immediately reveal to the observer that the man who here speaks to us was a fervent Catholic but also a fervent admirer of pagan beauty, and that in both images he spoke with equal authority as well as sincerity.

Transformations of pagan figures into Christian ones are numerous in the work of Rubens, and I shall later point out some outstanding examples, utilizing in several cases ancient models discussed before but supplementing them here and there with others not previously mentioned. But there were also transformations of pagan figures into other *pagan* figures, and these are, quite naturally, often subject to less change than are those used

[Fig. 31] Rubens, St. Sebastian. Berlin-Dahlem Museum

Rubens, Andromeda. Berlin-Dahlem Museum [Fig. 32]

for biblical characters. I shall therefore analyze a few of these first; in fact I have anticipated this with the example, discussed in the preceding chapter, of Tityos–Hippolytus–Prometheus.

The so-called *Venus of Doidalses* or *Crouching Venus* (Fig. 34) was familiar to Rubens from a Roman version in the Vatican. This marble was ingeniously transformed into the Ceres of a picture of 1613 in Kassel (Fig. 33)[2] which represents the popular quotation from Terence's *Eunuch:* (IV, 732) "Sine Cerere et Libero friget Venus" (Venus needs Ceres and Bacchus to warm herself), a favorite of several late Mannerist draftsmen and painters. While Rubens' Venus sits relaxed accepting the invigorating offerings of the god of wine and the goddess of the "cereals," the latter has assumed the crouching position and the unmistakable disposition of the legs which characterize the Hellenistic marble. The Kassel picture belongs to a group of works painted by Rubens somewhere between 1612 and 1615 which have shocked and baffled some writers because of their almost "ac-

[Fig. 33] Rubens, Venus, Bacchus, and Ceres. Kassel, Museum

ademic"-classicistic forms of a kind not found in works of the master's Italian period or of his later phases. It is evident[3] that they reflect an attempt on the part of Rubens to discipline himself, and very probably his first students as well, in the pursuit of most vigorous standards of firm and even compressed composition. This self-discipline was to bear fruit in the following years of exuberant and highly dramatic pictures, often of gigantic proportions.

It will be remembered that Rubens made many copies after the *Laocoön,* both of the whole group (Fig. 9) and of its single members. It is therefore no surprise to find many echoes of its constituent parts in later paintings of his.[4] More daringly still, Rubens combined two views of the elder son of Laocoön in the large *Ganymede* of about 1611 in the Prince Schwarzenberg Collection in Vienna (Fig. 35)[5]: the characteristic position of the two legs is here reproduced as drawn in the Ambrosiana copy, whereas the upper part of the body, the arms, and the head

[Fig. 34]
Venus. Rome, Vatican

Rubens, Ganymede.
Vienna, Prince Schwarzenberg Collection

[Fig. 35]

turned into profile are translated into the reverse, thus orienting the figure to the upper right where it finds its necessary compositional complement in the two divine messengers welcoming him to Olympus. Variations of this kind are much more subtle than the direct copies where no change in subject is involved. I have already mentioned some simpler examples of the latter type, but I am adding another here in order to make this phenomenon quite clear. When the mature master, in his allegory of the *Good Government of Marie de Medici* (Fig. 36), represented her reign as one sponsored by, and comparable to, that of the ancient gods themselves, it seemed imperative to make the figure of Apollo, who triumphs over the representatives of evil, unmistakable, and for that reason Rubens fashioned it closely on that of the image of Apollo known to all, namely the *Apollo Belvedere* (Fig. 37).[6] It is somewhat less clear why he should have painted Saturn, standing with his scythe on his arm and restrained by Mercury, as an almost exact repetition of an early

[Fig. 36] Rubens, Good Government of Marie de' Medici, *modello.* Munich, Alte Pinakothek

drawing in which he copied an ancient statue of the Arundel Collection supposed to represent Homer (Fig. 38),[7] but we can be sure that Rubens did not do this unintentionally; it is always safer to assume that we do not know the reason than that Rubens did so without reason.

We may conclude this discussion on adaptation of ancient figures to pagan subjects with a glance at one of Rubens' last, and perhaps least understood, paintings—the *Three Graces* in the Prado (Fig. 39).[8] Like practically all representations of this subject, Rubens' picture harks back to the famous Hellenistic group preserved in many copies, the best known in Siena (Fig. 40), which was discovered in Rome in the fifteenth century and was certainly familiar to Rubens. This marble had been the source of Raphael's early picture of the *Hesperides* (Fig. 41), and one could say that what the young Umbrian did was to give an ingenuous and graceful reconstruction of the antique trio. His cool colors, embellishing a flawless design, evoke the memory

[Fig. 37] Apollo Belvedere. Rome, Vatican

Rubens, "Homer." Berlin-Dahlem Museum [Fig. 38]

of an ivory group; his quiet landscape, of a soft enamel ground. Rubens saw in the ancient marble the germ of goddesses whose bodies vibrate with life, life from which life springs, and who are surrounded by nature in full bloom, a nature which conforms to the curves of their bodies; all thought of stone has been banished, and it is as though Rubens had wanted to give the perfect example of what he demanded of painters in his treatise on the imitation of ancient statues: "omnino citra saxum"—before all, avoid the effect of stone. In these last years of his life in particular, color was everything to Rubens, and this picture is indeed all color: in the luminosity of the bodies, in the incredible splendor of the deep green and pink touches of the distant landscape, and no less in the dynamic forms of branches, the discarded garments, the flowers and fountain. But equally important is the complete integration of idea and form. The goddesses of the ancient marble, and Raphael's picture as well, have only a *formal* center, not a psychological center at all.

[Fig. 39] Rubens, The Three Graces. Madrid, Prado

[Fig. 40] The Three Graces. Siena, Cathedral

The left and right figures look outside the circle with a dreamy expression; each is self-contained. They are three Graces; Rubens' alone are The Three Graces. They turn to each other, they smile at each other, they belong to each other, they touch each other with loving awareness of their warm bodies. The transformation from stone into pigment, from aloofness to happy union is complete.

In connection with translations of pagan subjects into biblical ones I should like to refer to the *Thornpuller* or *Spinario* (Fig. 42) now usually considered the work of a classicistic sculptor (of the Augustan age?) rather than a Greek master of the classical period. This statue survived the middle ages without having been christianized; but it was able to do so only as a symbol of various vices.[9] It is interesting to see that a touch of fascinated embarrassment persists in a copy by Jan Gossaert made as late as the early sixteenth century. We do not possess a copy of the *Spinario* by Rubens; but how little the subject would have em-

Raphael, Hesperides. Chantilly, Musée Condé [Fig. 41]

barrassed him can be gathered from the magnificent drawing in London (Fig. 43),[10] in which he had a youth "pose" as the *Spinario,* more or less exactly, in the figure on the right; more fully transformed into a boy drying his feet and looking at the spectator, in that on the left. It is this latter figure which was used for the young man drying his feet in the *Baptism of Christ,* the large canvas painted for the Jesuit church in Mantua about 1605, a preparatory drawing of which has been preserved (Fig. 44);[11] and this composition also contains an adaptation from the *Torso Belvedere,* in the old man struggling with his shirt (in the reverse position). But the *Spinario* also reappears in a freer version in a subject from the Old Testament where a young woman has been engaged in a similar action and where her attention is dramatically diverted to some unexpected happening close-by. This is the *Susanna,* in which the heroine, while bathing, is threatened by the two Elders, a work of the early Roman period

[Fig. 42] Spinario. Rome, Palazzo dei Conservatori

still in the Villa Borghese (Fig. 45)[12] and chronologically not far removed from the *Spinario* drawing.

Another transformation of special interest begins with the ancient statue of *Pudicitia,* which Rubens saw in Rome and which is now in the Vatican Museum (Fig. 46). A brief pen sketch of this is preserved in the Pushkin Museum in Moscow (Fig. 47), where the figure is seen in a three-quarter view, combined with another figure which was to emerge a little later (about 1614) as the Mary in a painting of the *Return from the Flight into Egypt,* now in the Atheneum at Hartford;[13] in fact, the other side of the same sheet contains a quick preparatory sketch for that painting (in reverse). The meaning of the *Pudicitia* in this context is not clear; but another painting of the same period, the *Holy Women at the Sepulchre* of the Czernin Collection (now in the Residenzgalerie, Salzburg, Fig. 48),[14] has taken over the figure in its entirety. However, here she does not represent the

Rubens, Youth in Pose of Spinario. London, British Museum [Fig. 43]

[Fig. 44] Rubens, Baptism of Christ. Paris, Louvre

[Fig. 46] Pudicitia. Rome, Vatican

Rubens, Pudicitia and Mary. Moscow, Pushkin Museum [Fig. 47]

Rubens, Susanna. Rome, Galleria Borghese [Fig. 45]

Rubens, Holy Women at the Sepulchre. Salzburg, Czernin Collection [Fig. 48]

allegory of chastity but a chaste woman from the closest entourage of Christ: one of the Holy Women looking for Christ's body in the tomb. Here, as in the *Apollo Belvedere* in the Medici Cycle, we have an exact copy, but this time it is a transfer from a pagan allegorical figure to a Christian saint. Is she a *particular* saint? It is hard to tell for certain, but I believe that Rubens followed here the account of St. Luke (24: 1-10), which expressly states (v. 10) that "it was Mary Magdalene, and Joanna, and Mary the mother of James, and other women, that were with them, which told these things unto the Apostles." This passage, and this one alone, puts Mary Magdalene into such a commanding position that I think it almost impossible to doubt that Rubens gave the most prominent role in this picture to her. And I feel I am justified in thinking that Rubens saw the sinner Mary Magdalene transformed into a *Pudicitia* by her faith in the Resurrection announced to her by the angels, just as a few years later he was to represent her as the main beneficiary of Christ's total forgiveness and acceptance in the subdued presence of the other penitents, St. Peter, King David, and the Good Thief, in that unforgettable painting in Munich.[15]

Another noteworthy example of the decidedly original use of works of ancient art in a Christian subject is found in one of Rubens' most powerful altarpieces commissioned to him soon after his return to Antwerp, *The Erection of the Cross* (Fig. 49). The modern placement of this huge panel in the transept of Antwerp Cathedral, opposite the *Descent from the Cross,* continues to create the false impression that the two works were intended as companion pieces. In actual fact only the *Descent* was painted for the Cathedral, whereas the earlier *Erection* was painted in 1610-11 for the high altar of the church of St. Walburga, since pulled down.[16] The triptych was originally crowned by a lunette in which one saw the half figure of God the Father about to receive the martyred body of Christ into Heaven; and the entire composition of the central painting is based upon the idea of that ascent which is seen as inseparable from the erection of the cross on which Christ first had to die, in other words, on the transmutation of the victim into the victor. In this way those responsible for the erection really labor for the *ascension,* and I am using the word "labor" advisedly because Rubens, following here in the footsteps of his greatest contemporary, Caravaggio, did not shrink from representing the muscular effort involved in raising the cross. However, the herculean bodies of the men assigned to this task labor in the chiaroscuro of the ground and thus do not divert our attention from Christ on whose body the light is concentrated.

It has always seemed to me that in depicting the scene just described Rubens utilized one from the *Gemma Augustea* (Fig. 6) which was drawn by him some time before 1621 (Fig. 7) and appears to have been known to him from casts or from painted copies long before that.[17] In the left part of its lower tier we see a group of soldiers erecting a *tropaion;* one keeps it on the ground while another pulls it up on a rope; one holds it in the middle, and a fourth puts his shoulder against its top; under it are seated two prisoners, a dour-looking barbarian and his plaintive wife.

Rubens, Erection of the Cross. Antwerp, Cathedral [Fig. 49]

The pattern of the pulling procedure and the main actors place this very close to Rubens' interpretation; but I also feel that the soldier in Rubens' painting who puts his back against the cross between the two main herculean bodies is a transformation of the prisoner in the cameo who simply sits below the trophy;[18] he was welded into the group of straining men by Rubens who could not tolerate a passive figure as a part of the main scene and therefore shifted all onlookers to the wings of the triptych. But the whole adaptation was again far from being a mere formal transposition; what rises before us in Rubens' painting is a trophy of a different kind, now actively witnessed and received by the August Ruler above.

Among the Christian saints, St. George is perhaps the one who comes closest to the classical conception of the hero: the possessor of physical beauty and prowess, the destroyer of a monster, the chivalrous protector of a virgin—these are the same virtues which had made the ancient heroes the paragons of medieval aristocracy. As a female saint by Rubens has the beauty of an Andromeda and the dignity of a Thusnelda, his male saints, and St. George on horseback in particular, have the strength, the heroic cast, and in early works often the sheer dash of both Perseus and Marcus Curtius. Correspondingly, the royal daughter whom St. George rescued from the dragon, was seen as a worthy and equally virtuous successor to Andromeda who was liberated by Perseus.

It is no surprise to see this tradition reach an early culmination in Rubens' magnificent painting of about 1606-07, now in Madrid (Fig. 50), and to find that his virgin was patterned almost exactly after an ancient statue.[19] The latter had become known to Rubens either in the original or in an engraving published in Rome in 1585, in which the original was reproduced in reverse (Fig. 51); Rubens had already made use of it in a figure being disrobed for baptism in a preparatory drawing for the *Baptism of Christ* which I adduced for its other copies from antiquity (Fig. 44). It is surprising that the ancient statue should present *Leda Caressed by the Swan,* and one may wonder about Rubens' use of such a figure, first for a convert to Christian baptism and then for the virtuous daughter of a king. But to the archaeologists and artists of the Renaissance and the Baroque, Leda was anything but a frivolous girl flirting with Jupiter disguised as a swan. Not only was she the innocent victim of Jupiter's cunning, as was eloquently expressed in the interpretation given her by Michelangelo (which, incidentally, was copied by Rubens),[20] but she was also, and perhaps primarily, the revered mother of the Dioscuri, Castor and Pollux, the angel-like messengers of the supreme divinity, the protectors of sailors from danger at sea and—what is certainly not without significance in connection with this picture—great horsemen, as Rubens was to show in a painting to be discussed presently. Royal personages of the late sixteenth century could receive no higher honor than representation in the guise of Castor and Pollux. Pierre de Ronsard prescribed it for the Dukes of Anjou and of Alençon in his program for the *Entrée Triomphale* of Charles IX of France.[21] A Leda-princess was just the right kind of person to be liberated by the Christian Knight, St. George.

[Fig. 50] Rubens, St. George. Madrid, Prado

Leda, engraving of 1585, reversed [Fig. 51]

I have endeavored to show that in the art of Rubens transformations of pagan figures into Christian ones are not arbitrary. Occasional remote reminiscences may reflect merely formal stimuli, but this never happens where content really counts. It is of course not accidental that most of my examples, and here I include transformations from pagan models into *pagan* figures, were taken from works of his Italian and early Antwerp periods; it is in these that the process is still clearly discernible, whereas in later works the connections often appear more vague, the influences too subtle to be identified. But they never ceased to be an important part of his art.

Naturally, there are cases in which Rubens availed himself of neither ancient nor recent models of any kind in rendering classical subjects but relied almost entirely on his own thorough knowledge of literary sources, his own understanding of the human body, and his own unlimited imagination. But these cases are actually rare. Rubens, like Händel, was the *Vollender*

[Fig. 52] Rubens, Daughters of Leucippus. Munich, Alte Pinakothek

of a great tradition rather than a rebel against tradition; and the extent of his originality in the face of unending borrowing remains one of the most extraordinary phenomena in the history of art. Even a number of seemingly free inventions turn out to be related to ancient art in subtle ways when carefully investigated.

For one such example I am returning once more to the Dioscuri, Castor and Pollux, of whom I have just written in connection with the Leda-like appearance of St. George's princess. In Rubens' brilliant painting of about 1617 in Munich (Fig. 52), these shining knights are seen abducting two beautiful maidens, Hilaira and Phoebe, the daughters of King Leucippus of Messenia.[22] Our consideration of this work must exclude a detailed extended analysis of the greatness of this abduction scene as a *composition:* that great rotation of action and reaction, of pulling and repelling, all contained within a sunlike circle from which emanate protuberances of celestial fire and energy.

The Dioscuri. Rome, Quirinal [Fig. 53]

There is no precedent for this theme in painting. Abductions of all kinds were popular, but this one occurs only on a few ancient sarcophagi in a form that has no bearing on Rubens' interpretation, and in book illustrations, where the Dioscuri do appear mounted but without their quarry. There exist a few other abduction scenes in which horses appear, but the relation of Rubens' picture to them is quite remote. Ancient vase paintings of the subject were hardly known to Rubens, and they, too, differ fundamentally from his.[23] The story is told by Theocritus in the twentieth Idyl, and much later by Ovid in his *Fasti* (V, 699), and by Hyginus (*Fabulae,* 80). It was not a popular story with the literati either; in fact, the real subject of the painting had been entirely forgotten and mistaken for a *Rape of the Sabine Women* until the great German novelist, critic, and Rubens connoisseur extraordinary, Wilhelm Heinse, rediscovered it in 1777 on a visit to the Düsseldorf Gallery after having by chance reread his Theocritus on the same day.[24]

I mentioned before that the Dioscuri were famous for their accomplishments as horsemen. According to the ancient sources this was primarily true of Castor, while Pollux was praised as the great boxer; Castor was sometimes given the bit of a horse as an attribute. But in the course of time both became recognized as great horsemen, and this fact was sanctioned, as it were, by the large statues erected to the twins and their horses in Rome. These were brought to the *Monte Cavallo*—so named for them—of the Quirinal by Sixtus V in 1589 and given their final position by Pius VI in 1787 (Fig. 53). The great horses were among the most celebrated sights of Rome, more so almost than the figures of the brothers. The groups are Hadrianic copies of fifth-century Greek originals (one is optimistically inscribed Phidias, the other Praxiteles) and have fascinated artists throughout the centuries, from Pisanello, Donatello, Mantegna all the way down to Hans von Marées in the nineteenth century.[25] Rubens' acquaintance with them is proved by at least one of his drawings.[26] Thus, his decision to make the Dioscuri abduct the girls on their horses was dictated not by his literary source and even less by pictorial tradition but by a logic nourished by memories of the greatest and most widely known monument of the Dioscuri. This was blended with the exigencies of an unfolding visual pattern regarding the new subject, that is, the abduction, the violence of which seemed most fittingly expressed by the rearing motion of the horses; and even the typically Rubensian *containment* of that violence within a tightly defined circle was to a degree suggested by the interrelationship of figures and horses on the Quirinal.

In this light we may perhaps also re-evaluate the audacity of the subject matter and its appropriateness as a pictorial theme. The Dioscuri were, after all, demigods whose behavior was not regulated by normal rules. When, according to one version, Castor was about to be killed by the slighted fiancé of one of the princesses, Jupiter interfered in his favor.[27] To be chosen by these heroes, the benevolent protectors of a large part of mankind, must have been esteemed a great honor by the two maidens. Theocritus reports that the Dioscuri had bribed Leucippus to deliver his daughters into their hands; this explanation was clearly scorned by Rubens, who in contrast to the representation on all Greek vase paintings admitted no crowds to the scene, let alone a cunning Leucippus. His interpretation lends it the dignity of a rite: four wonderful, youthful bodies are united in a love struggle over which none of them seems to have control but which is seen in terms of an orderly cosmos, indeed a tightly circumscribed world in which nothing counts or even happens but that central event; the only witnesses are the little cupids who are really the prime movers of it all but who stick discreetly to their task as assistants rather than proudly exulting over what they have wrought.[28]

Another very rare mythological subject of Rubens is the *Finding of Erichthonius,* the story of the little monster with the serpent tail, earth-born after Vulcan's frustrated pursuit of Minerva, handed by her for discreet safe keeping to the daughters of Cecrops, and uncovered by Aglauros who could not control her curiosity. I have recently traced the iconography of this subject prior to Rubens in some detail;[29] it must suffice here to say that his representations bear practically no relationship to any older work. I shall also be brief on his own two paintings which have been most lucidly discussed by Ludwig Burchard.[30] The first, in the Liechtenstein Collection in Vaduz (Fig. 54), was painted about 1616 and is a prime example of Rubens' ability, and tendency at that time, to supplement a narrative by allegorical elements throwing light on basic attitudes and connotations of the participants. The old woman, who is not mentioned by any text, may have been added by Rubens simply in order to enh nce the beauty of the young girls. However, the putto above e basket, who incidentally was patterned after an antique figure n a sarcophagus in Pisa, fulfills the same function as the cupids in the *Leucippides,* namely the enhancement of the action by allegorical allusions which add to the liveliness of the scene—in this case by mischievously inviting the reluctant and somewhat frightened sister on the left to join the fun. In an earlier "state" of the same picture, known to us from an engraving made immediately after its completion, a second putto,

[Fig. 54]

Rubens, Finding of Erichthonius.
Vaduz, Prince Liechtenstein Collection

flying up over the old nurse, trumpeted the event; this was obliterated by Rubens himself and replaced by the crow of the ancient tale. By the same token, the fountain on the right allegorically indicated the presence of Gaia, the mother of the little monster, in the form of *Artemis Ephesia,* an antique figure dear to Rubens and often interpreted as *Terra* in his time.[31]

The old nurse is likewise a beautiful asset to Rubens' late rendering of the subject, painted about 1635, of which the Oberlin Museum owns the only surviving fragment (Fig. 55). Many old copies of this apparently very famous canvas have come down to us (Fig. 56), and Burchard was able to reconstruct from them two different "stages" of the original; an oil *modello* for the composition, now with the Duke of Rutland at Belvoir Castle, is a very close anticipation of its first state. Rubens has here significantly altered the mood of the Liechtenstein painting. There is now no putto egging the sisters on, no excited dog, no crow tattling, no allusion to the mother of the

Rubens, Finding of Erichthonius. Oberlin, Allen Memorial Art Museum

[Fig. 55]

After Rubens, Finding of Erichthonius. Columbus, Georgia, Mayo Collection

[Fig. 56]

monster; not even a hesitation remains. Behind the intimate, relaxed group stretches a garden architecture with two quiet herms; the fountain, now of equally "neutral" design, permits a glimpse of a serene, very Titianesque landscape. This is an idyl, not a story; but it is a thoroughly antique idyl.

We have been mostly concerned with mythological subjects,[32] and it is time now to consider briefly the cycle by Rubens which deals with an event of Roman history: the story of the Consul Decius Mus. We shall leave his most famous cycle of paintings, the one treating the life of Marie de' Medici, to the next chapter since it has to do, not with an ancient story, but with a modern one though seen *sub specie antiquitatis.*

For the story of Decius Mus, Rubens had no pictorial tradition whatever to lean on. This does not mean that he did not utilize older patterns of form and content for its individual actors; but on the whole, he was on his own.

When Sir Dudley Carleton suggested to Rubens that he look for a series of tapestries which might constitute part of the group of works he hoped to receive for his collection of antique marbles, Rubens wrote him on May 26, 1618:[33] "In regard to the tapestries I can say little because, to tell the truth, there are no very fine pieces at present; and as I have already written, they are rarely to be found unless made to order. Since that history of Camillus did not satisfy Your Excellency, it seemed to me that the one of Scipio and Hannibal, to which your agent did not appear disinclined, might perhaps please Your Excellency more. To tell the truth, the choice is arbitrary among these things, which are all without doubt of great excellence. I will send Your Excellency all the measurements of my cartoons of the history of Decius Mus, the Roman Consul who sacrificed himself for the victory of the Roman people; but I must write to Brussels for the exact figures, since I have consigned everything to the master of the factory." Carleton did not wait for this to materialize, but the reference to the Decius Mus cartoons by Rubens himself is of great value to us because even in the oldest references this series was given erroneously to van

Dyck. In an earlier letter of May 12, 1618,[34] Rubens did not define the subject of the tapestry series but undoubtedly referred to the same set, and from this source we learn that it had been ordered by "certain Genoese gentlemen" (probably of the Pallavicini family) and that they were being worked on when the letter was written. The large paintings from which the (lost) cartoons proper were made (presumably in water color) are now in the Liechtenstein Gallery in Vaduz. There are six of them, pertaining to the story of the Consul's heroic death, and it is possible that the young van Dyck, then (1617) an advanced associate rather than an apprentice of Rubens, did have a share in their execution but certainly not in their invention. Some oil sketches that have survived are undoubtedly by Rubens himself.

The story of Decius Mus has been told by Livy (VIII, 6-9). The Roman troops, opposing the Samnites, were led by Decius Mus and Manlius Torquatus; Rubens eliminated the latter. Before the battle Decius Mus had a dream: the gods demanded that of the two armies one would have to sacrifice its commander, the other itself in its entirety. Rubens' first picture represents the Consul divulging this oracle to his officers in the traditional form of the *adlocutio,* known from reliefs and coins. A sacrifice then reveals to the priests that the army sacrificing its commander will conquer. In the third picture Decius Mus devotes himself to death; in the fourth he dispatches the lictors to notify his coconsul; in the fifth he plunges into the thick of battle, restoring the courage of his troops; in the sixth he is placed on the bier in solemn preparation for his cremation.

The cycle belongs to the least known and studied works of Rubens, although Jacob Burckhardt[35] and Hans Gerhard Evers[36] have written some fine pages about it. Burckhardt said that it is "infused with a deep and genuine feeling for the greatness of Rome, such as David and his successors, for instance, never attained with all their rhetoric." A full justification of this claim would require a discussion of the whole series, and that is impossible here; I must restrict myself to a single panel, the oil *modello* now in the Kress Collection at the National Gallery in

Washington (Fig. 57), which was used without change in the final version but for the elimination of the eagle above the Consul. As I mentioned before, the general pattern of an *adlocutio* was accessible on ancient coins and reliefs; it is also possible that Rubens knew and utilized a famous painting by Titian, which in turn had made use of antique precedents: the *Allocution of the Marchese del Vasto,* painted in 1540 and today in the Prado in Madrid (Fig. 58).[37] However, Titian had to adapt the ancient model or models to a piece of *contemporary* history; Rubens had to adapt the ancient model to a *different* piece of *ancient* history, and it is evident that he squarely faced the challenge of this subject as an archaeologist and historian as well as an artist.[38] Like Leopold Ranke two hundred years later, he asked himself "how the things actually occurred," and although in other historical renderings he hardly ever hesitated to blend history with allegory—I shall return to this principle—he seems

[Fig. 57] Rubens, Decius Mus Addressing the Legions, *modello.* Washington, D.C., National Gallery of Art

to have forced himself in this series to do without allegorical allusions; this is possibly the reason for his later omission of the eagle which in the *modello* allegorically represented Rome.

And yet, freedom of interpretation remained one of Rubens' paramount concerns. This is not Livy illustrated, it is a drama in six acts based on Livy. Whether addressing his troops, realizing the meaning of the sacrifice, being consecrated to death, saying farewell to the lictors, seeking death in battle, or lying in state victorious—it is the hero himself who receives our full attention. If this is the most purely Roman work of the master it is not because he wished to be more of a historian than an artist; it is because the story of Decius Mus, never before represented in art, was for him the very epitome of Roman greatness and liberated in him new artistic impulses which enabled him to bestow unexcelled artistic grandeur upon the most exalted of Roman virtues.

Titian, Allocution of Marchese del Vasto. Madrid, Prado [Fig. 58]

IV. The Past and the Present

It remains for us to investigate what it was that produced the wealth of adaptations and transformations of the classical tradition in Rubens' works. What was the driving force behind that prodigious artistic activity which has confounded many to the point of refusing to credit a single person with the enormous ingenuity necessary for adapting and transforming a heritage of such immense scope? Perhaps we can understand this better if we discuss at somewhat greater length two points: first, the extent to which this tradition permeated every aspect of Rubens' art and second, the extent to which it permeated his whole personality and extra-artistic activity.

I have already stressed that in the representation of Christian themes and characters Rubens utilized his vast repertory of forms derived from ancient art with complete assurance; they underwent the same alterations and readjustments as did his adaptations of them for classical subjects, no more and no less, and eventually achieved the same subtle transformation, in which the *spirit* rather than the actual forms of ancient art remained. That this identity of the pagan and Christian spheres was a deeply rooted conviction there cannot be the slightest doubt. I have mentioned before that this attitude was one of the basic phenomena of the reaction against the oppressive tendencies and regulations of the Counter-Reformation, and that in conquering that dichotomy by recognizing and reviving the more liberal point of view of the great High Renaissance masters Rubens expressed the attitude of a whole generation although certainly as its leader. To the juxtaposition of *St. Sebastian* and *Andromeda* mentioned before (Figs. 31 and 32) I should like to add that of the *Slaughter of the Innocents* in Munich (Fig. 59) and the *Rape of the Sabines* in London (Fig. 60), both very late works, possibly painted in the same year (about 1635), both large glowing pictures painted on wood, both entirely done by Rubens' own hand.[1] Classical references abound in both, either based directly on ancient works such as the *Laocoön* soldier in the *Innocents,* or on Rubens' earlier adaptations such as the *Daughters of Leucippus,* which provided the model for the Roman abducting a Sabine woman on horseback. But more important still to our present quest is the fact that the central figures of both compositions, the despairing mother here and the entreating Sabine matron there, wear contemporary costumes. Rubens thus deliberately and almost ostentatiously made these subjects scenes of his own time and, with that, expressed the cruel truth that the martyrdom of the mothers of unjustly slain babies and of the women violated in the pursuit of political struggle were not just stories from the past.

Such conversions of stories from the past, both biblical and classical, were of course not new. Christian allegorization of classical subjects had in fact been the only possible means of keeping the latter alive in the middle ages; without the substitution of either the Virtuous Soul or the Devil for the Apollo of the pursuit of Daphne[2] we would have no medieval representations of that particular Ovid story. By the same token, any medieval rendering of the Passion or other stories from the life of Christ or of the saints indicates that the painters saw their subjects in terms of contemporary, that is, timeless events, the more so as they saw them constantly enacted in that fashion in mystery plays. On the other hand, the Renaissance had put an end, at least in art on a high level, to this kind of naïve realization. The ancient myths had regained their independence and integrity; the classical text in its pristine form had triumphed over the Christian commentaries and *integumenta,* the nude body over the priestly or virginal guise. To be sure, in Christian subject matter the Renaissance masters had made no attempt to reconstruct the biblical costumes and other accoutrements in reliable forms (this was to be the dubious prerogative of the nineteenth century), but the most obtrusive everyday features had been eliminated and a dignified, often classical-inspired ambience established. Rubens' injection of deliberately contemporary features, though not without Mannerist antecedents, is part of a highly original conception of allegory which played a decisive role in his works and made a lasting impression on other Baroque artists. However, although in the examples of the *Slaughter of the Innocents* and the *Sabine Women* the contemporary note is inserted into scenes which on the whole retain the Renaissance concept of stories in their own right, and although in many cases Rubens did not introduce any allegorical meaning at all but concentrated entirely on the action proper, his achievements were even greater in what one might call the reverse process: the representation of *contemporary* subjects with the vitalizing insertion of allegorically interpreted motifs from the classical past.

A characteristic example is one of the most lovingly conceived pictures of his late years, the incomparable *Garden of Love*, in

[Fig. 59] Rubens, Slaughter of the Innocents. Munich, Alte Pinakothek

Madrid (Fig. 61).[3] Here are lovers of Rubens' time and environment, all in contemporary costumes, shown in happy union, and presented in a chain of groups expressing various stages of persuasion and consent, in a rhythm of such superlative beauty that it established a pattern for all subsequent *Gardens of Love,* from Watteau on down. Their place of assembly, however, is the Garden of Venus with her temple and its statues and fountain figures, and although the discreet hostess herself is absent her messengers are not: one of them gives a gentle push to a reluctant maiden, others frolic with the central group in anticipation, and others hover in the air strewing flowers and generally welcoming the visitors to their haunt. They are the progeny of the cupids we found active in the *Daughters of Leucippus* (Fig. 52), aiding and abetting Castor and Pollux, and inviting mischief in the early *Finding of Erichthonius* (Fig. 54). In the latter we were able to point to their specific source, whereas in the late work in the Prado they have become creations of such spontaneity

Rubens, Rape of the Sabines. London, National Gallery [Fig. 60]

that it would be foolish to look for direct borrowings from the past. Yet they are spirits from the past still *actively affecting* our most intimate thoughts and actions.

In the *Garden of Love* the synthesis of modern life and classical allegory is apparently of an entirely impersonal nature; it is impossible to recognize individuals, including even Rubens' second wife, Hélène Fourment, *pace* those who, as Goethe's Mephistofeles says, "see Helena in every woman." However, classical allegory applied to specific events and persons seems to have fascinated Rubens at a very early stage of his career, long before it reached its climax in the *Medici Cycle.*

I have already mentioned briefly a picture rediscovered in 1965 in the Prague Castle Gallery (Fig. 62). The author of the article in which this important find was published, Jaroslav Neumann,[4] has analyzed the picture with great acumen and his complicated exposé carries conviction in all its main points. At first sight, the painting represents nothing more than a rather

[Fig. 61] Rubens, Garden of Love. Madrid, Prado

lively argument on Mount Olympus. Evidently Juno, on the left, makes some substantial accusations against Venus, who is standing on the right. Minerva supports Juno; Apollo, seated on a sphinx in a spectacular pose, defends Venus. The positions in the heated discussion are illustrated by the rendering, behind Juno, of a sedate elderly couple, embodying legitimate love under the protection of the goddess of marriage, and, behind Venus, of Ceres and Bacchus in an illicit embrace. These are the main points and figures of the picture, which is crowded with auxiliary actors and packed with reminiscences, not so much from ancient works as from those by Mantegna and Giulio Romano, Rubens' greatest predecessors at the court of Mantua. Now Neumann has pointed out that Mount Olympus was the emblem of the Gonzaga; that the river god with the swan stands for the Po; that Juno wears a contemporary costume; and, most importantly, that the picture is filled with astronomical details and astrological allusions. The allusions are achieved with the

Rubens, Strife on Mt. Olympus. Prague, Castle Gallery [Fig. 62]

help of the identification of the gods with their appropriate "houses," such as the Fishes behind Venus, which provide an exact date for the painting, namely the year 1602-03. That this must be a more or less disguised allegory of a special event in the life of Rubens' patron, Duke Vincenzo of Gonzaga, cannot be doubted; whether he liked it is a different question—the picture seems to have been put in storage with some alacrity. To show a ruler in the act of making a difficult moral choice was common practice, as is proved by many identifications of such persons with *Hercules in bivio,* that is, Hercules choosing between Virtue and Vice;[5] but what we have here points to the choice between matrimony and free love—and one may perhaps suspect that this created a touchy situation.

The fusion of contemporary events with allegory based on the classical past has never been handled with greater power and skill than in Rubens' *Medici Cycle.*[6]

The relationship between Rubens and Marie de' Medici is one of the most extraordinary examples of friendship between a great artist and a great patron; unfortunately, its documentation is spotty. Rubens first saw the young Medici princess when she was married by proxy to Henri IV in her native Florence in 1600; the young painter had joined his prince, the Duke of Mantua, as a witness to the ceremony. In January, 1622, Marie de' Medici called Rubens to Paris to talk over with him her ambitious plans for the decoration of her new Luxembourg Palace. Marie had ruled France after the assassination of her husband in 1610; in 1617 she had clashed with her son, sixteen-year-old Louis XIII, had been exiled to Blois until 1619, but reinstated to the Council in 1621. Her final defeat at the hand of Richelieu was not to come until 1630, when she was exiled to Compiègne; and although she escaped once more a year later, she became an embittered expatriate for the rest of her life and tried in vain to enlist the help of the Spaniards, the United Provinces, and others for a struggle with Richelieu. Rubens, whom she outlived by two years, was her most faithful friend and, in fact, tried hard to persuade the powers that be in Brussels to promote her plans; if this was a mistake (and who knows for certain whether it was?), it was a mistake founded on a touching loyalty. Rubens' lack of love for Richelieu was hardly due only to the cardinal's dubious artistic taste (he later was to show the depths to which his much vaunted connoisseurship could sink by recommending to replace Rubens with Cesare d'Arpino for the gallery of Henri IV).

Two large galleries at the Luxembourg Palace were to be decorated, one with twenty-one canvases representing scenes from the life of the queen, the other with a series of pictures from the life of her late husband, Henri IV. This second cycle was begun by Rubens soon after he had completed the first (1625) but only sporadically continued, and after Marie's banishment in 1630 it was abandoned; nevertheless, some magnificent sketches and the underpainting of some of the large canvases have survived.[7]

The series of twenty-one scenes from Marie's life are today installed in the Louvre, in a hanging approximating their original one. In them, events from her life or outright allegories of facets of her character are universalized by being wedded to classical concepts. True, this is she—but it is also all of us. The view that the cycle is a courtier's uncritical glorification of a princely patron is utterly without foundation. An unbiased observer will instead find an extraordinary kaleidoscopic representation of the human pageant, done with tact and wit as well as great power, always full of sparkle and élan, and very different from the often vapid allegories painted by Mannerists such as Vasari. From the overture, in which the destiny of Marie is being woven by the Three Fates under the watchful and benevolent eyes of Jupiter and Juno, to the coda in which Time carries the Revealed Truth upward to the reunited images of Marie and her husband, events develop rapidly under the constant surveillance of the gods, but the tragic episodes of Marie's life are not omitted. All scenes are viewed *sub specie universali.*

Her education, for instance (Fig. 63), is an enchanting evocation of classical education in general, and that it is she, a princess, who receives it, does not make it less interesting or less universally valid. She is a little girl, as are many others, and her privilege is not unique if we understand Rubens' allegorical language correctly; it had been his own and that of many of his friends, and it is of the value of that education that he speaks to us, a priceless heritage to be carefully preserved. Minerva instructs her in the fundamentals of learning, Apollo in music, painting, and sculpture, Mercury in economics; the Three Graces watch over her growth and her manners; all this takes place in a cool grove before the waters of the Castilian Spring. The enraptured attitude of Henri IV viewing Marie's portrait offered him by Hymenaeus and a cupid under the benevolent glances of the divine sponsors of marriage, Jupiter and Juno (Fig. 64), is depicted with a wonderful sense of humor which raises it far above the kind of impersonal adulation encountered in most comparable representations.

The allegory of Marie's happy reign (Fig. 36), mentioned before because of its prototypes in ancient statuary, is of course not without hyperbole; but we must realize that Rubens was

[Fig. 63] Rubens, Education of Marie de' Medici, *modello.* Munich, Alte Pinakothek

not entirely free in establishing the program of this cycle and had to follow guide lines prescribed by the Abbé de St. Ambroise, Marie's foremost adviser; in this light the universal note given most of the canvases is even more remarkable. It is a real surprise to see that neither the queen nor her adviser opposed including the allusions to her temporary exile at Blois, even if this was done through the representation of her *escape* from the castle, and to her quarrels with her son represented by the shaky Treaty of Angoulème,[8] renewed hostilities, and the final reconciliation. It is true that a projected representation of the queen leaving Paris for her exile was discarded. But this elimination does not seem to have displeased Rubens at all; we must not forget that he was a very sincere and loyal admirer of the queen, and that he became tired of the life at her court not because of her but because of Richelieu, whom even then he seems to have deeply distrusted.

On May 13, 1625, Rubens wrote a letter to Peiresc which I

Rubens, Henri IV Viewing the Portrait of Marie de' Medici, *modello*. Munich, Alte Pinakothek [Fig. 64]

am quoting in part not only because it mentions this particular matter but also because of its indication of how astutely Rubens managed to say almost exactly what he wanted to say with this series in spite of some interference: "His Majesty showed complete satisfaction with our pictures, from the reports of all who were present, particularly M. de St. Ambroise. He served as interpreter of the subjects, changing or concealing the true meaning with great skill. I believe I've written you that a picture representing 'The Departure of the Queen from Paris' has been removed, and in its place I have painted an entirely new one, representing 'The Felicity of Her Regency.' This shows the flowering of the Kingdom of France, with the revival of the sciences and the arts through the liberality and the splendor of Her Majesty, who sits upon a shining throne and holds a scale in her hands, keeping the world in equilibrium by her prudence and equity. This subject, which does not specifically touch upon the *raison d'état* of this reign, or apply to any individual, has evoked much pleasure, and I believe that if the other subjects had been entrusted entirely to us, they would have passed, as far as the Court is concerned, without any scandal or murmur . . . "[9]

The *Medici Cycle* does not stand alone, and it is possible to find comparable characteristics and ideas in several other scenes from contemporary history which Rubens conceived in analogous terms. This is true of the *Apotheosis of James I of England* painted by the master for the ceiling of the Banqueting House at Whitehall, London, in the early 1630's,[10] and of the paintings inserted by him in the triumphal arches erected in Antwerp in 1634-35 for the solemn entry of the new stadholder of the Southern Netherlands, the Cardinal-Infant Ferdinand of Spain. A word on the latter must suffice. Rubens had by then retired from diplomatic service and lived a quieter life with his new young family, mostly in the castle Het Steen on his country estate between Antwerp and Malines. But he was persuaded to participate in the festivities planned for that event, primarily out of reverence for the memory of Ferdinand's eminent predecessor, Rubens' beloved friend and patroness, Archduchess Isabella, who had died late in 1633. The master himself took a prominent part in the literary program, made sketches for a large number of the canvases, and even seems to have painted (or at least retouched) several with his own hand, although he was already being sorely plagued by arthritis.

Fortunately, many of his preliminary oil sketches and modellos have survived, and although we have to rely chiefly on the printed illustrated report and its engravings for an appreciation of the ensemble effect of the triumphal arches, each individual panel among those sketches tells a story of undiminished artistic greatness and undiminished imagination and verve in transforming into living, dynamic events what would have been cold, allegorical contrivances with most other painters.[11] For the *Quos Ego!,* with which Neptune calms the impudent winds symbolizing the perils of one of Ferdinand's sea voyages, Rubens made a sketch of the greatest beauty (Fig. 65),[12] now in the Fogg Art Museum of Harvard University and perhaps the most enchant-

Rubens, Quos Ego!, *modello*.
Cambridge, Mass., Fogg Art Museum [Fig. 65]

ing Rubens sketch in this country. Here every figure—the wrathful Neptune, the wild wind gods, the frantic nymphs, the neighing steeds—is in itself an incomparable *allegro con brio,* and in conjunction with the dim vision of a great sailing fleet, a seemingly unlimited expanse of sea and threatening clouds, they form an ensemble of overwhelming atmospheric unity and concerted action. The sketch is a superb example of a complete re-embodiment of the classical past in a vibrant present.

Rubens' palatial house in Antwerp which he acquired and rebuilt during the second decade of the seventeenth century has been restored to much of its old dignity with the aid of reliable reproductions.[13] It reflects the fact, which by now should not surprise anyone, that Rubens was a gifted architect on the side; an enthusiastic admirer of the early Baroque architecture he had encountered in the city of Genoa during his Italian years and of its more recent development; the author and publisher, at his own cost, of a precious illustrated volume on those Geno-

[Fig. 66] Antwerp, Rubens' House, entrance to studio

ese palaces.[14] As we approach the studio (Fig. 66) we find the architecture decorated with a meaningful ensemble of statues and busts. On the lower level a satyr, faun, Pan, and Silenus hold sway; they are the symbols of pulsating life, of fertility, and of the *flatus divinus;* in many works of the master they had received, and were to receive, a place of great dignity while at the same time reveling in their animal powers. Above the door there is the bust of Seneca, the hero and martyr of the stoic faith and the ancient philosopher whom Rubens most admired. Higher up, there are some of Seneca's great forerunners and one successor: Socrates, Plato, Sophocles, and Marcus Aurelius; still higher up, the gods themselves: Mars, Juno, Jupiter, and Vesta. As we stand before the splendid garden pavilion we are confronted with a portico (Fig. 67) bearing statues of Minerva and Mercury, whom we encountered earlier as the educational tutelaries of young Marie de' Medici, and busts of a satyr and a satyress. And here, between ancient symbols of the physical

Antwerp, Rubens' House, portico [Fig. 67]

prowess of man and woman, we find inscribed these verses from Rubens' favorite poet, Juvenal: "Leave it to the gods to give us what is fit and useful to us; dearer to them is man than he is to himself. One must pray for a healthy mind in a healthy body, for a courageous soul which is not afraid of death . . . [and] which is free of wrath and desires nothing."

The last sentence (Orandum est ut sit mens sana in corpore sano. Fortem posce animum [et] mortis terrore carentem . . . Nesciat irasci, cupiat nihil; *Sat.*, X, 356-360) is Rubens' classical credo which merged magnificently and convincingly with his Catholic Christian creed. This was a blend made possible by a new equilibrium between religious and secular thought which was produced by the regained ecclesiastic position of strength and the concomitant liberalization of thought. Rubens' stoicism was nourished by that of Juvenal and of Seneca and by his own religion; but it was a stoicism vastly more optimistic than Juvenal's and more worldly-wise than that of the Church. And it was fired by a desire on the part of the artist which has little or no precedence in either Juvenal or even Seneca and theological stoicism: the unquenchable desire to serve humanity at large, to promote peace and sanity among men.[15] I am now turning to this most personal aspect of Rubens' world view.

Among the great artists who sacrificed a large part of their creative life to moral concerns and who would have stood speechless before those contending that an artist exists for the sake of "self-expression," Dürer and Rubens stand out in lonely greatness: Dürer as a writer and teacher, a veritable *praeceptor Germaniae et mundi*, the first great thinker among northern artists, the creator of a new language not only in images but also in prose;[16] Rubens as a diplomat who served his superiors, yes, but even more the cause of peace as he saw and felt it, and did not hesitate to go his own way. He was a diplomat of decisive importance in the European affairs of his time, the forger of a durable peace between Spain and England. His only profound disappointment in this field was his inability to reconcile the two sister peoples of the southern and northern Netherlands—a task, incidentally, which has not been brought to an entirely satisfactory conclusion to this day.

One feels that only a double wellspring could have provided Rubens with the strength to live up to this incredible load, this double existence as one of Europe's most sought-after and most productive artists and as one of Europe's most respected and successful diplomats, the person of whom the excellent Ambrogio Spinola said that painting was really but the least of his accomplishments.[17] Undoubtedly, one source of this strength was that inseparable unity of the Christian and the classical tradition that was his and his only among the great Baroque painters. But this alone would have availed little if it had not been supplemented by a unique sense of responsibility. He not only *professed* the dogma of free will and *quoted* the highest examples of virtue in the ancient world; he was *inspired* by them to serve mankind as a peacemaker while at the same time tirelessly extolling the paradigms of Christian and classical heroism and grandeur in images which drew their inspiration from both realms in a spirit of free interchangeability.

Little more than two years before Rubens' death, on March 12, 1638, the artist wrote to his fellow countryman, Justus Sustermans, court-painter to the Duke of Tuscany, a letter known to us from a reliable copy. It contains one of the very few descriptions and explanations Rubens ever made of a painting of his own (a painting probably commissioned to him by the Tuscan court), the kind of allegory which Jacob Burckhardt proposed to call "moralities" (Fig. 68): "As for the subject of the picture, it is very clear, so that with the little I wrote to you about it at the beginning, the remainder will perhaps make itself better understood to your experienced eye, than through my explanation. Nevertheless, in order to obey you, I will describe it in a few words. The principal figure is Mars, who has left the open temple of Janus (which in time of peace, according to Roman custom, remained closed) and rushes forth with shield and blood-stained sword, threatening the people with great disaster. He pays little heed to Venus, his mistress, who, accompanied by her Amors and Cupids, strives with caresses and embraces to hold him. From the other side, Mars is dragged forward by the Fury Alekto, with a torch in her hand. Nearby are monsters personifying Pestilence and Famine, those inseparable partners of War. On the ground, turning her back, lies a woman with a broken lute, representing Harmony, which is incompatible with the discord of War. There is also a mother with a child in her arms, indicating that fecundity, procreation, and charity are thwarted by War, which corrupts and destroys everything. In addition, one sees an architect thrown on his back with his instruments in his hand, to show that that which in time of peace is constructed for the use and ornamentation of the City, is hurled to the ground by the force of arms and falls to ruin. I believe, if I remember rightly, that you will find on the ground under the feet of Mars a book as well as a drawing on paper, to imply that he treads underfoot all the arts and letters. There ought also to be a bundle of darts or arrows, with the band which held them together undone; these when bound form the symbol of Concord. Beside them is the caduceus and an olive-branch, attribute of Peace; these also are cast aside. That grief-stricken woman clothed in black, with

[Fig. 68] Rubens, The Horrors of War, *modello*. London, National Gallery

torn veil, robbed of all her jewels and other ornaments, is the unfortunate Europe who, for so many years now, has suffered plunder, outrage, and misery, which are so injurious to everyone that it is unnecessary to go into detail. Europe's attribute is the globe, borne by a small angel or genius, and surmounted by the cross, to symbolize the Christian world. That is as much as I can tell you, and it seems to me too much, because with your sagacity, you will have understood it easily . . ."[18] To this, the aging master, as mindful of his responsibilities and as urbane as ever, added the following postscript: "I am afraid that a fresh painting, after remaining so long packed in a case, might suffer a little in the colors, particularly in the flesh tones, and the whites might become somewhat yellowish. But since you are such a great man in our profession, you will easily remedy this by exposing it to the sun, and leaving it there at intervals. And if need be, you may, with my permission, put your hand to it and retouch it wherever damage or my carelessness may render it necessary. And once more I kiss your hands."

V. Rubens and the Classical Tradition in the Eyes of Later Critics

We may now consider how our subject appears in the literature on Rubens and how these interpretations reflect the time and the personalities to which they belong.[1]

French classicistic art theory of the seventeenth and early eighteenth centuries as centered at the Academy of Painting and Sculpture had a special interest in Rubens' ideas about the antique because of the struggle, within its own ranks, between the "Poussinists" and the "Rubenists." Since, according to one of the Academy's main aestheticians, without the ancients "everything is blind and rank barbarism"[2] much depended on the correct definition of what antiquity really stood for. André Félibien, following the line of the leading Italian theorist of the advanced Seicento, Giovanni Pietro Bellori, undertook to prove to the *Rubenists* that their idol was all wrong in his interpretation of antiquity.[3] To be sure, Rubens was an admirer and collector of ancient art, but he made the wrong use of it in his own work. Félibien[4] singled out the Medici Cycle as an example of Rubens' ineptness in this regard. Yes, he was a great painter; yes, there are splendid things in the Medici Cycle. But when the author's fictitious companion complains: "What, I ask you, have Cupid, Hymen, Mercury, The Graces, Tritons and Nereids to do in the History of Henri IV and Marie de' Medici? And what is the connection between the gods of the fables and the ceremonies of the church and our customs which justifies this painter's joining them together and confusing them the way he did in the works you have just discussed?" the author meekly replies that this is indeed an abuse which cannot be too strongly condemned and which Rubens ought to have avoided more than any other painter, "since he had studied so much."

But according to Bellori and Félibien, Rubens' main fault was that even when he used pagan subjects proper he used them in the wrong way, not in what Félibien called the "antique" way, namely one employing "perfect form"; and with this reproach we are back where it all started. The "perfect form" is Poussin's, and Rubens is not Poussin; on the contrary, he uses distorted forms deliberately. Thus, Rubens' contour with all its vivacity and vitality is scorned because it did not accord with Poussin's; it was irregular, hence wrong.

The leader of the *Rubenists,* Roger de Piles,[5] had the good sense to quote, in defense of his party, Rubens himself, namely his treatise *De imitatione statuarum,* from which I included a few passages in my second chapter, and another, apparently lost treatise by Rubens on the beauty of ancient art. However de Piles convinced only those who were already on his side. These people did have some feeling for inspiration in great art although, like Dürer, they by no means underrated the rational element, occasionally even to excess. It is a sobering fact that this defender of Rubens' greatness, of his freedom in the treatment of ancient models and of his color, should have been the same Roger de Piles who in his *Balance des peintres* graded all great artists of the past and present by numbers from zero to twenty according to four categories of excellence in painting. In this process, Caravaggio came out with a 0 in expression, a 16 in color, a 6 in design, and a 6 in composition, while Charles Lebrun received a 16 in expression, an 8 in color, and a 16 in both design and composition.[6] Nevertheless, his enthusiasm for Rubens was great (he received, together with Raphael, the highest total score in the *Balance:* a 17 in expression, a 17 in color, a 13 in design, an 18 in composition); his view of Rubens is sympathetic and intelligent, and his estimation of Rubens' relationship to antiquity, just and positive; he even anticipated much of the attitude of Winckelmann and Goethe when he said that Rubens "made painting more vivid and more natural, as it were, than nature itself."[7] He was more enlightened in this respect than almost all eighteenth-century French writers, including those of the Enlightenment. Then, even those who defended Rubens because he turned to nature rather than to plaster casts misunderstood his relationship to the classical past; they simply thought that he had repudiated the ancients and left it at that.

An important change occurred only at the time, and in the circle, of the great German critics of the late eighteenth and early nineteenth centuries. The distinction between the French classicistic tradition of the seventeenth century and the revolutionary classicism of Winckelmann cannot be better illustrated than by a comparison of the two attitudes toward our problem. Winckelmann had the great good sense to realize Rubens' stature; he praised his treatment of all-permeating light which he contrasted with what he called the "impudent way of painting with deep shadows"[8] (a thrust not only at Caravaggio but also at Giorgione and Ribera); following Roger de Piles he said that Rubens "stands *above* nature and treats it with a view toward *his superior aims.*"[9] As to the master's relationship to the classical tradition, he says that Rubens, although "far removed from the Greek contour of the body,"[10] is not below the level of ancient art. And here we even find the first comparison of Rubens with Homer, for Rubens had a similarly "inexhaustible fertility" of imagination, and he painted his women strong and powerfully built as did Homer, and also Zeuxis. He was "the Michelangelo of his century."[11] Shades of Félibien! It is only here that Rubens' similarity to, rather than dependence upon antiquity is asserted.

While we find merely scattered remarks on Rubens by Goethe—he, like Winckelmann, stressed the point that Rubens, being a great artist, stands *above* nature[12]—Wilhelm Heinse, whom I have already cited as the discoverer of the correct subject of the *Abduction of the Daughters of Leucippus,* stands out as one of the most gifted of all writers on Rubens. His *Berichte aus der Düsseldorfer Gemäldegalerie,* written 1776-77,[13] belong with the finest pieces of art criticism, and those who have read Heinse's magnificent novel *Ardinghello* will realize that his sympathy for Rubens stemmed from a passionate zest for life which found ample nourishment in Rubens' art even though he was apt to overlook, perhaps, the noble restraint of Rubens' sensuality.

But what a pen! In the faces of the Leucippides (Fig. 52) he detected a "duel between morality and nature," and the body of one of them "hovers like a rose at the moment of being gathered" (schwebt wie eine Rose im Gepflücktwerden). This was seen with an artist's eye, and Heinse fully realized the significance of the *action* of the cupids and, with that, of one of Rubens' most important visual devices. Heinse saw in Rubens a *true Greek* because he was able to see Greek art with Rubens' eyes. The same judgment had already been made in a book (published anonymously) by an otherwise practically unknown author by the name of J. G. B. von Wichmannshausen (1769), who had called Rubens truly Greek because he imitated nature rather than statuary.[14] An important point in the discussion of the subject "Rubens and the Classical Tradition" was reached when Johann Heinrich Merck, writing in 1778, recognized in the late *Crucifixion of St. Peter* in St. Peter's, Cologne, a work which at first sight seems to be the epitome of violence, an example of Rubens' wise compositional restraint (dass Rubens dem Feuer seiner Imagination mit Weisheit habe zu gebieten gewusst).[15] This was a discovery unparalleled in the minds of the Romanticists and their philosophic advisers. Not until Jacob Burckhardt was this discerning insight expressed again.

Among the influential German art historians who were slowly working their way out of the fetters of philosophical systems, Heinrich Gustav Hotho[16] stands out by virtue of his deep and almost unqualified reverence for Rubens. Rubens is for him, as he had been for Heinse and Wichmannshausen, the Greek artist par excellence, but he provides a more reasoned demonstration of this judgment. Sculpture was the ideal art of the Greeks; it expresses to perfection the physical element. Painting (not drawing which borders on the sculptural) was the ideal art of Rubens; it expresses to perfection the spiritual element, nearly as fully as does music. But in this very difference lies the correlation of the two because their *interests* often coincide. Rubens' love of the nude expresses something of decisive importance to the Greeks but through his own totally different means; he knows how to express exuberance as did Greek sculptors (and again

Homer) but again through his own totally different means. This new spirituality through painting is at the same time seen by Hotho as a station on the way to *purely* spiritual art; in this respect he is a Hegelian like many others, but of a rare kind: one with eyes discovering first, and with the mind acting on the visual data later.

And it was eyes, and this time the artist's eyes, that directed and inspired the tongue of the only two great French writers on Rubens in the nineteenth century, Delacroix and Fromentin. Their eulogies of Rubens were preceded by those of Henry Fuseli who in 1801 wrote the beautiful words: "Rubens was endowed with a full comprehension of his own character."[17] Delacroix[18] took up Winckelmann's characterization of Rubens as the Homer of painting; Fromentin spoke of that "soul truly open to all things—happy, confident, and great"[19] and of the fact that "his life is in full light; it is broad daylight there as in his pictures";[20] also of "the fortifying and healthful hygiene of his genius";[21] "his was a soul without storms, or languors, or torments, or chimeras";[22] the *Raising of the Cross* (Fig. 49) is "conceived, conducted, scanned, illuminated like the proudest verses written in Pindaric form."[23] Here speaks the Frenchman with a classical education *and* with the artist's sensitivity, not the successor of Félibien.

The pragmatic approach of most of the art-historical research in the second half of the nineteenth and early twentieth centuries did not favor discussion of our topic on a broad basis but yielded a number of important factual studies, including Goeler von Ravensburg's book of 1882[24] and Franz Haberditzl's extensive article of 1911-12.[25] They were augmented later by Emil Kieser's two articles of 1933 and 1938-39,[26] which signified an important advance toward the solution of the more difficult problems. More recently Ludwig Burchard, Julius Held, Michael Jaffé, Justus Müller Hofstede, and others have enlarged our knowledge with important new investigations.[27]

But with this we have run far ahead of Jacob Burckhardt's great work on Rubens which was written in 1896 and only posthumously published in 1898. I have already expressed my belief that Burckhardt's book on the master, whom he called one of the greatest in the history of art and at the same time a "completely luminous" personality, is still the finest of all;[28] it would perhaps have had a peer if Georg Graf Vitzthum had been granted the opportunity to write his book before his premature death. Burckhardt and Vitzthum were the only great writers and lecturers who understood and formulated the full truth of Merck's groundbreaking insight of the *aristocratic restraint* in Rubens—so utterly different from the popular image and not sufficiently appreciated even by Delacroix[29]. Burckhardt expressed it beautifully when he wrote that "the horses of his sun chariot are fiery creatures, but he would not let them run away with it"[30]—and this in spite of the fact that "it was as if religion, princely power, saga, the myth and poetry of all times, his own family and the circle of close friends, even elemental nature, both in the animal kingdom and in landscape, had turned confidingly to him that he might take them on his eagle's pinions."[31] Although the reminiscent old Burckhardt of the *Erinnerungen* spoke of Rubens as a basically unanalyzable phenomenon, a true hero, "creative in full analogy to nature," he did imply that the restraint in the art of this "northern executor of the Renaissance," that "perfect marriage between the Renaissance and the spirit of the Germanic and the Romance north,"[32] was the fruit of the classical heritage as understood, revered, and made fully his own by a great and "luminous" genius.

Notes

CHAPTER I. THE LITERARY AND ARCHAEOLOGICAL HERITAGE

1. Basel, 1898, reprinted in the *Gesamt-Ausgabe,* XIII (Stuttgart-Basel, 1934), 367ff, and singly, 1928 (Leipzig) and 1938 (Vienna). Written chiefly in 1896. Emil Maurer, *Jacob Burckhardt und Rubens* (Basel, 1951), pp. 130ff.

2. Ed. H. Gerson, trans. M. Hottinger (London: Phaidon Press, 1950).

3. Basel, 1905; in English as *Force and Freedom; Reflections on History,* ed. J. Hastings-Nichols (New York, 1943).

4. *Recollections,* p. 1.

5. *Recollections,* pp. 156f.

6. *Kunstgeschichtliche Grundbegriffe* (Basel, 1915); in English as *Principles of Art History,* trans. M. Hottinger (London, 1932).

7. On this problem, see L. Becherucci, "Mannerism," *Encyclopedia of World Art,* IX (1959), cols. 443ff, with full bibliography.

8. See the letter of April 5, 1875, to Max Alioth, quoted by W. Waetzoldt, *Deutsche Kunsthistoriker* (Leipzig, 1924), II, 199; in English in *The Letters of Jacob Burckhardt,* trans. A. Dru (New York, 1955), p. 164.

9. Particularly in his early period; see the article "Über Murillo. Kunststudien aus dem Louvre," written in Paris in 1843 and published by H. Zeeck in *Atlantis,* IX (Zürich, 1937), 481ff; in 1845, he called Murillo "the first painter of his century" (J. Gantner, *Schönheit und Grenzen der klassischen Form,* Vienna, 1949, p. 19).

10. See the lecture given on Nov. 6, 1877 *(Gesamt-Ausgabe,* XIV, 178ff), and the quotations in Waetzoldt, *Deutsche Kunsthistoriker,* II, 189 and 203f. J. Gantner, "Jacob Burckhardts Urteil über Rembrandt und seine Konzeption des Klassischen," *Concinnitas* (Basel, 1944), pp. 83ff. On the contemporary background of this critical attitude toward Rembrandt see Werner Kaegi, *Europäische Horizonte im Denken Jacob Burckhardts* (Basel-Stuttgart, 1962), pp. 147ff.

11. *Recollections,* p. 1.

12. *Magurn, Letters.*

13. *Magurn, Letters,* pp. 32ff; on the change in the quotation from Horace see Martin Warnke, *Kommentare zu Rubens* (Berlin, 1965), p. 75, n. 30.

14. That it was painted in the same spirit of personal allegory as the *Strife on Mount Olympus* (see Chapter IV and Fig. 62) is not certain but very probable. The composition exists in two painted versions: a smaller one in the Yale University Collection (apparently once owned by Rembrandt) and a larger one in Dresden; a drawing, attributed to L. Vorsterman, is in the Louvre. That the picture originated during the Mantua period cannot be doubted. See M. Jaffé, "Rubens in Italy: Rediscovered Works," *Burlington Magazine,* C (1958), 411ff, esp. 419ff.

15. J. Held, "Rubens and Virgil," *Art Bulletin,* XXIX (1947), 125f. (The translation is by Theodore C. Williams.) The subject reoccurs in Claude Lorrain's last painting (1682). For another extremely rare subject, *Meleager Killing his Uncles,* see *Burchard-d'Hulst* (1963), no. 83. For the *Daughters of Leucippus* see Chapter III and Fig. 52.

16. For the original text see *Correspondance,* VI, 179ff; *Magurn, Letters,* p. 407.

17. First published by H. Hymans in *Bulletin de l'Académie royale des sciences, des lettres et des beaux-arts de Belgique,* third ser., XIII (1887), 150ff.

18. P. Humbert, *Un amateur: Peiresc, 1580-1637* (Paris, 1933).

19. *Magurn, Letters,* pp. 365ff.

20. E. Kieser, "Antikes im Werke des Rubens," *Münchner Jahrbuch der bildenden Kunst,* n.s., X (1933), 110ff, particularly p. 136.

21. *Magurn, Letters,* pp. 90ff.

22. *Correspondance,* III, 85ff. My translation is from the Italian text which is reprinted, together with an unreliable English translation, in D. Dubon, *Tapestries from the Samuel H. Kress Collection at the Philadelphia Museum of Art* (1964), p. 6.

23. F. Lugt, "Rubens and Stimmer," *Art Quarterly,* VI (1943), 99ff; *Held, Drawings,* I, 53ff.

24. *Held, Drawings,* I, 51. An elaborate study of all Rubens drawings after the antique is being prepared by M. van der Meulen-Schregardus.

25. *Held, Drawings,* I, 47; on the question of Rubens' originals in this group see J. Müller Hofstede, "Beiträge zum zeichnerischen Werk von Rubens," *Wallraf-Richartz-Jahrbuch,* XXVII (1965), 259ff, especially 274ff (some of these views have already been opposed by other writers).

26. *Magurn, Letters,* pp. 59ff.

27. *Magurn, Letters,* p. 63.

28. *Correspondance,* II, 190ff.

29. S. Speth-Holtershoff, *Les Peintres flamands de cabinets d'amateurs au XVIIe siècle* (Brussels, 1957), pp. 119ff and fig. 49; a detail is reproduced in *Rooses 1904, p. 152.*

30. *Correspondance,* II, 192.

31. M. C. Ross, "The Rubens Vase—its History and Date," *Journal of the Walters Art Gallery,* VI (1943), 9ff.

32. *Magurn, Letters,* pp. 263ff.

33. C. Norris, "Rubens and the Great Cameo," *Phoenix,* III (1948), 179ff (p. 180 and fig. 4).

34. *Magurn, Letters,* pp. 111ff.

35. *Correspondance,* III, 365, 371; Norris, "Rubens," p. 180.

36. Norris, "Rubens," p. 179 and fig. 1.

37. *Correspondance,* p. 443.

38. *Magurn, Letters,* pp. 132ff.

39. *Correspondance,* II, 290.

40. Norris, "Rubens," p. 180 and fig. 6.

41. *Correspondance,* III, 183ff.

42. *Magurn, Letters,* p. 111.

43. *Held, Drawings,* I, 50.

44. *Ibid.*

45. *Ibid.; Glück-Haberditzl,* nos. 28ff.

46. *Magurn, Letters,* pp. 320ff.

CHAPTER II, ADAPTATION

1. *Held, Drawings,* I, 49ff.

2. See E. K. J. Reznicek, *Die Zeichnungen von Hendrick Goltzius* (Utrecht, 1961), I, 89ff and 321ff.

3. *Fubini-Held.*

4. *Fubini-Held,* pl. 1.

5. *Fubini-Held,* fig. 8; *Burchard-d'Hulst,* no. 15.

6. *Fubini-Held,* pls. 2-4.

7. London, National Gallery; *KdK* 315. Now called "Studio of Rubens," but surely retouched and "accepted" by him.

8. It has been assumed that Rubens worked from a plaster cast of the *Notte.* See the careful entry in C. van Hasselt and A. Blankert, *Artisti olandesi e fiamminghi in Italia* (from the Coll. F. Lugt) (Florence, 1966), no. 40.

9. *Exh. Amsterdam 1933,* no. 93.

10. J. Müller Hofstede, "Beiträge zum zeichnerischen Werk von Rubens," in *Wallraf-Richartz-Jahrbuch,* XXVII (1965), 288; no small bronze of the *Torso* has as yet been found. On the possibility of recognizing Philoctetus in this statue see A. Andrén, "Il Torso del Belvedere," *Opuscula Archaeologica,* VII (1952), 1ff, and W. Helbig, *Führer durch die öffentlichen Sammlungen . . . ,* 4th ed. (Tübingen, 1963), pp. 211ff.

11. E. K. J. Reznicek (See n.2), I, 321f, nos. 201-202; II, figs. 156-157.

12. First published by its then owner, Roger de Piles, in *Cours de peinture par principes* (Paris, 1708), pp. 139ff.; F. Goeler von Ravensburg, *Rubens und die Antike* (Jena, 1882), pp. 195ff; M. Warnke, *Kommentare zu Rubens* (Berlin, 1965), pp. 106ff; M. Jaffé, *Van Dyck's Antwerp Sketchbook* (London, 1966), pp. 16ff, 301ff.

13. Roger de Piles, *Abrégé de la vie des peintres,* 2nd ed. (Paris, 1715), pp. 391ff; I am quoting from the English translation in *The Art of Painting* (London, 1744), p. 258 (which has the misprint "irregularity" for "regularity").

14. *Exh. Amsterdam 1933,* no. 92.

15. *Ibid.,* no. 94.

16. *Fubini-Held,* pl. 5. It is very enlightening to compare this drawing with the copy of the same view of the statue drawn in 1639 by Pieter van Lint (C. van Hasselt and A. Blankert, *Artisti in Italia,* no. 33.

17. U. Kuznetsov, "Drawings by Rubens from the Museums in the USSR" (text in Russian) 1965, no. 7, pl. 1.

18. Rotterdam, Museum Boymans-van Beuningen, Cat. 1962, no. 1760a.

19. *Fubini-Held,* pl. 9a. See *ibid.,* p. 141 and pl. 9b on a most deceptive copy of Rubens' copy in Copenhagen.

20. *Glück-Haberditzl,* no. 26; Kuznetsov (see n.17 above), no. 4.

21. Gisela M. A. Richter, *The Portraits of the Greeks* (London, 1965), I, 58ff.

22. *Goris-Held,* no. 101; *Exh. Fogg-Morgan 1956,* no. 13, pl. XVII.

23. Karlsruhe and Antwerp, Museum Plantin-Moretus; see Cat. Karlsruhe, Kunsthalle, 1966, p. 259, no. 178.

24. *KdK* 44. I cannot agree with Martin Warnke (*Kommentare zu Rubens,* Berlin, 1965, pp. 25ff) when he sees this picture as a *criticism* of Seneca's attitude toward death; Christian objections to radical stoicism certainly existed, but this picture does not belong in that context.

25. *Fubini-Held,* pl. 6.

26. V. H. Miesel, "Rubens' Study Drawings after Ancient Sculpture," *Gazette des Beaux-Arts,* ser. 6, LXI (1963), fig. 2; Kuznetsov (see n.17 above), no. 5. For a rear view see *Pantheon, XXV* (1967), 219.

27. *Exh. Fogg-Morgan 1956,* no. 5, pl. II; *Held, Drawings,* I, 156ff, no. 160.

28. E. Kieser, "Antikes im Werke des Rubens," *Münchner Jahrbuch der bildenden Kunst,* n.s., X (1933), 110ff, particularly pp. 117ff.

29. *Glück-Haberditzl,* no. 100.

30. *Exh. Fogg-Morgan 1956,* no. 27, pl. XVII; *Exh. Antwerp 1956,* no. 130. See also Rubens' copy of a full-length statue of "Nero" in the Lugt Collection (van Hasselt—Blankert, see n.8 above, no. 41); the marble was later in Earl Arundel's collection and is now in the British Museum.

31. A strange picture in a private collection in London, attributed to Rubens by M. Jaffé (*Burlington Magazine,* IC, 1957, 432) and by J. Müller Hofstede (*Wallraf-Richartz-Jahrbuch,* XXVII, 1965, 281ff) and not known to me in the original, contrasts the depravity of Nero with the upright sobriety of Seneca in a daring juxtaposition. While the surface of this picture looks disquieting in a good photograph, its "unattractive" way of expressing a moral judgment through unrelenting physiognomical characterization inspires confidence.

32. *Fubini-Held,* p. 137 and pl. 8.

33. *Fubini-Held,* pl. 7.

34. Reznicek (see n.2 above), no. 204 and pl. 159.

35. *KdK* 180; detail: *Fubini-Held,* fig. 11.

36. In Rotterdam and in the Lugt Collection; van Hasselt-Blankert (see n.8 above), no. 42.

37. *Glück-Haberditzl,* no. 25; *Burchard-d'Hulst,* no. 161 (as a late, corrected counterproof of an early drawing). The attribution of the marble to Montorsoli has been doubted by M. Jaffé, "Rubens as a Draughtsman," *Burlington Magazine,* CVII (1965), 372ff, esp. 381; he suggested an antique core.

38. M. Jaffé, "Rubens and Raphael," *Studies in Renaissance and Baroque Art Presented to Anthony Blunt* (London, 1967), pp. 98ff (the paper includes suggestions concerning Rubens' study of Raphael in the pre- and post-Italian periods as well).

39. M. Jaffé, "Rubens as a Collector of Drawings," *Master Drawings,* II (1964), 383ff, and III (1965), 21ff.

40. F. Kimball, "Rubens' *Prometheus,*" *Burlington Magazine,* XCIV, (1952), 66ff; J. S. Held, "Prometheus Bound," *Philadelphia Museum of Art Bulletin,* LIX (1963), 17ff.

41. Charles Dempsey, "Euanthes Redivivus: Rubens's *Prometheus Bound,*" *Journal of the Warburg and Courtauld Institutes,* XXX, (1967), 420ff. The change in the position of the legs on which I have commented in the text is the deliberate result of Rubens' careful reading of Tatius' text: "He . . . lifts up his thigh; but to his own harm, for this does but bring the bird nearer to his liver."

42. Prado, no. 1693.

43. J. Walker, *Bellini and Titian at Ferrara* (London, 1956), pp. 80ff and 105ff.

44. Walker, *Bellini and Titian at Ferrara,* pp. 80ff.

45. Francisco Pacheco, *Arte de la Pintura* (completed in 1638), ed. F. J. Sánchez Cantón (Madrid, 1956), I, 153 ("copió todas las cosas de Ticiano que tiene el Rey").

CHAPTER III. TRANSFORMATION

1. Painted ca. 1612 and ca. 1638-1640, respectively, and hanging together in the Museum at Berlin-Dahlem.

2. *KdK* 63.

3. Still of basic importance to this difficult problem is the article by R. Oldenbourg, "Die Nachwirkung Italiens auf Rubens und die Gründung seiner Werkstatt," *Jahrbuch der kunsthistorischen Sammlungen des allerhöchsten Kaiserhauses,* XXXIV (1918), reprinted in *Peter Paul Rubens,* ed. W. von Bode (Munich-Berlin, 1922), pp. 58ff.

4. See, for instance, H. von Einem, "Rubens' 'Abschied des Adonis' in Düsseldorf," *Wallraf-Richartz-Jahrbuch,* XXIX (1967), 141ff.

5. *KdK* 39; *Burchard-d'Hulst,* p. 32.

6. *KdK* 254.

7. H. Kauffmann in *Oud Holland,* XLVIII (1931), 197; *Exh. Antwerp 1956,* no. 10; *Burchard-d'Hulst,* no. 12.

8. *KdK* 434.

9. W. S. Heckscher, s. v. *Dornauszieher, Reallexikon zur deutschen Kunstgeschichte,* IV

(1958), cols 289ff; *idem, Sixtus IIII Aeneas insignes statuas Romano populo restituendas censuit* (The Hague, 1955), 14ff and 20ff. The Gossaert drawing is illustrated in the former.

10. *Glück-Haberditzl*, no. 27; *Burchard-d'Hulst*, no. 16, pp. 34ff; dated in the late Roman years by J. Müller Hofstede, "Beiträge zum zeichnerischen Werk von Rubens," *Wallraf-Richartz-Jahrbuch*, XXVII (1965), 271.

11. *Glück-Haberditzl*, no. 50.

12. *KdK* 19; *Burchard-d'Hulst*, p. 35.

13. M. Jaffé, " 'The Return from the Flight into Egypt' by Peter Paul Rubens," *Wadsworth Atheneum Bulletin*, 5th ser., no. 8 (Summer 1961), pp. 10ff.

14. *KdK* 79; Cat. Salzburg 1955, no. 109.

15. *KdK* 176.

16. *Rooses 1904*, I, 129; *Evers 1942*, p. 128.

17. This derivation has also been suggested by E. Kieser, "Antikes im Werke des Rubens," *Münchner Jahrbuch der bildenden Kunst*, n.s., X (1933), 115.

18. There may also be a connection with a sarcophagus now in Princeton (*Held, Drawings*, I, 129), but it seems to be of lesser significance to me.

19. J. Müller Hofstede, "Rubens' St. Georg und seine frühen Reiterbildnisse," *Zeitschrift für Kunstgeschichte*, XXVIII (1965), 69ff, particularly 76 and 78, figs. 6 and 7.

20. Rubens' copy is in the Dresden Gallery; *Evers 1942*, fig. 47.

21. P. Blanchemain, *Oeuvres inédites de P. de Ronsard, gentilhomme vandomois* (Paris, 1855), p. 48; W. Stechow, *Northern Renaissance Art, 1400-1600, Sources and Documents* (Englewood Cliffs, N.J., 1966), p. 160.

22. *KdK* 131.

23. A. Furtwängler in W. H. Roscher, *Ausführliches Lexikon der griechischen und römischen Mythologie*, I (Leipzig, 1884-1886), cols 1173ff.

24. *Sämtliche Werke* (Leipzig, 1904), IX, 340; also reprinted in: Wilhelm Heinse, *Vom grossen Leben*, ed. R. Benz (Munich, 1943), pp. 116ff.

25. E. Hubala in *Reallexikon zur deutschen Kunstgeschichte*, IV (Stuttgart, 1958), cols 47ff.

26. *Held, Drawings*, I, 116, no. 52 (Berlin drawing of a *Roman Triumph*, datable ca. 1622); cf. also the Copenhagen copy mentioned there.

27. See Bethe in Pauly-Wissowa, *Real-Encyclopädie*, V (Stuttgart, 1905), col. 1115.

28. Svetlana L. Alpers, "Manner and Meaning in some Rubens Mythologies," *Journal of the Warburg and Courtauld Institutes*, XXX (1967), 272ff, comes to hand just before this book goes to press. It is a highly significant contribution, but I believe that its author underestimates the narrative and dramatic elements in the works she discusses, in favor of an all too exclusive emphasis on the allegorical ones. When she says (p. 273) that "Castor and Pollux . . . have seized Hilaira and Phoebe . . . only to support and hold them poised in a great pattern against the sky" and to see the picture as an allegory of Marriage, she fails to evaluate properly Burckhardt's decisive insight into Rubens' restraint in rendering dramatic subjects and to do justice to his desire to *unite* such restrained drama with allegory. The same is true of her treatment of the Erichthonius picture at Vaduz (see the following paragraph in my text and fig. 54).

29. W. Stechow, "The Finding of Erichthonius: An Ancient Theme in Baroque Art," *Studies in Western Art (Acts of the Twentieth International Congress of the History of Art) III* (Princeton, 1963), 27ff.

30. L. Burchard, "Rubens' 'Daughters of Cecrops,' " *Allen Memorial Art Museum Bulletin*, XI (1953-1954), 4ff.

31. On the preparatory oil sketch for this picture, in Count Seilern's collection, see the article cited in n.29, this chapter.

32. One of the greatest manifestations of Rubens' genius in this field, the cycle of pictures from the *Metamorphoses* of Ovid painted after 1636 for the Torre de la Parada,

one of the hunting lodges of Philip IV of Spain, can only be mentioned here. They are the subject of a special study which Mrs. Svetlana Alpers of the University of California at Berkeley is preparing for publication.

33. *Magurn, Letters,* pp. 65ff.

34. *Magurn, Letters,* pp. 61ff.

35. *Recollections,* pp. 108ff.

36. *Evers 1942,* pp. 180ff. See also E. Kieser in *Münchner Jahrbuch der bildenden Kunst* (1933), pp. 126ff.

37. E. Panofsky, "Classical Reminiscences in Titian's Portraits: Another Note on his 'Allocution of the Marchese del Vasto,'" *Festschrift für Herbert von Einem* (Berlin, 1965), pp. 188ff.

38. On the relative accuracy of the armor in this composition, in contrast with Rubens' usually freer adaptations, see also H. D. Rodee, "Rubens' Treatment of Antique Armor," *Art Bulletin,* XLIX (1967), 223ff.

CHAPTER IV. THE PAST AND THE PRESENT

1. *KdK* 378 and 379.

2. W. Stechow, *Apollo und Daphne,* Studien der Bibliothek Warburg, no. XXIII (Leipzig-Berlin, 1932), and rev. ed. (Darmstadt, 1965), pp. 1ff.

3. *KdK* 348.

4. J. Neumann, "Z mladych let Petra Pavla Rubense" (with German summary), Umění XIII (1965), 541ff. Color reproduction in *L'Oeil,* December 1965. See also J. Neumann, *Die Gemäldegalerie der Prager Burg* (Prague, 1966), pp. 243ff.

5. E. Panofsky, *Hercules am Scheidewege und andere antike Bildstoffe in der neueren Kunst,* Studien der Bibliotek Warburg, no. XVIII (Leipzig-Berlin, 1930), pp. 117ff.

6. A. Beucler, *Rubens, La Galérie de Médicis* (Paris, 1935); O. von Simson, *Zur Genealogie der weltlichen Apotheose im Barock* (Strassburg, 1936); *idem,* "Richelieu and Rubens," *Review of Politics,* VI (1944), 422ff.

7. Ingrid Jost, "Bemerkungen zur Heinrichsgalerie des P. P. Rubens," *Nederlands Kunsthistorisch Jaarboek,* XV (1964), 175ff.

8. In which, according to von Simson, "Richelieu and Rubens," 438ff, Richelieu is shown in a highly ambiguous role.

9. *Magurn, Letters,* pp. 107ff.

10. Oliver O. Millar, *Rubens: The Whitehall Ceiling,* Carlton Lectures on Art, no. 40 (London-New York, 1958).

11. *Evers 1942,* pp. 369ff.

12. *Exh. Fogg-Morgan 1956,* no. 43, pl. XXIX.

13. *Evers 1942,* pp. 150ff; on its present state, see F. Baudouin, *Rubens House,* 3rd ed. (Antwerp, 1964).

14. *Palazzi di Genova . . .* (Antwerp, 1622).

15. On the role of Justus Lipsius in this development see Martin Warnke, *Kommentare zu Rubens* (Berlin, 1965), pp. 36ff.

16. E. Panofsky, *The Life and Art of Albrecht Dürer* (Princeton, 1955), pp. 242ff.

17. *Evers 1942,* p. 69.

18. *Magurn, Letters,* pp. 408ff.

CHAPTER V. RUBENS AND THE CLASSICAL TRADITION IN THE EYES OF LATER CRITICS

1. For the following survey I owe much to: O. Bock von Wülfingen, *Rubens in der deutschen Kunstbetrachtung* (Berlin, 1947), and V. H. Miesel, "Rubens, Ancient Art, and the Critics," *Criticism,* V (1963), 214ff.

2. Charles du Fresnoy (1668), quoted by Miesel, "Rubens," p. 216.

3. Miesel, "Rubens," p. 217.

4. *Entretiens sur les vies et les ouvrages des plus excellens peintres anciens et modernes,* second ed. (Paris, 1688), II, 211.

5. Miesel, pp. 218ff; J. Rosenberg, *On Quality in Art* (Princeton, 1967), pp. 31ff.

6. Translated in E. Holt, *A Documentary History of Art* (Garden City, N. Y., 1958), II, 185ff.

7. Roger de Piles, *Recueil de divers ouvrages sur la peinture et le coloris* (Paris, 1775), p. 271.

8. From *Beschreibung der vorzüglichsten Gemälde der Dresdner Galerie* (1753), quoted by Bock von Wülfingen, *Rubens,* p. 28.

9. *Ibid.*

10. Quoted *ibid.* from *Gedanken über die Nachahmung der griechischen Werke . . .* (1755).

11. See Bock von Wülfingen, *Rubens,* pp. 29-30.

12. *Gespräche mit Eckermann,* April 18, 1827; Bock von Wülfingen, p. 58.

13. Bock von Wülfingen, p. 46.

14. *Abhandlungen über die Mahlerey und Zeichnung* (Leipzig, 1769); Bock von Wülfingen, pp. 35ff.

15. "Notizen von einer malerischen Reise nach Köln, Bensburg und Düsseldorf," *Teutscher Merkur* (1778); Bock von Wülfingen, p. 53; Miesel, pp. 223ff.

16. *Geschichte der deutschen und niederländischen Malerei* (Berlin, 1842); Bock von Wülfingen, pp. 99ff; Miesel, pp. 228ff.

17. *Lecture on Painting* (London, 1801), p. 91; Bock von Wülfingen, p. 44.

18. *Journal de Eugène Delacroix,* ed. A. Joubin (Paris, 1950), III, 43.

19. *Les Maîtres d'autrefois* (first published at Vienne in 1876, here cited from the reprint, Paris, 1938), p. 56; English ed.: *The Old Masters of Belgium and Holland,* trans. M. C. Robbins (Boston, 1882), p. 54.

20. French ed., p. 106; English ed., p. 102.

21. French ed., p. 105; English ed., p. 101.

22. French ed., p. 107; English ed., p. 103.

23. French ed., p. 74; English ed., p. 71.

24. *Rubens und die Antike* (Jena, 1882).

25. "Studien über Rubens und die Antike," *Jahrbuch der Kunstsammlungen des allerhöchsten Kaiserhauses,* XXX (1911)12), 276ff.

26. "Antikes im Werke des Rubens," *Münchner Jahrbuch der bildenden Kunst,* n.s., X (1933), 110ff; *idem,* "Rubens' Münchner Silen und seine Vorstufen," *ibid.,* XIII (1938-39), 185ff.

27. See the notes to chapters I - IV of this book.

28. See Chapter I.

29. "His painting, in which imagination dominates, is superabundant throughout . . . His picture resembles a gathering in which everyone talks at once"—and yet, at the end of the same paragraph, he returns to Rubens' praise: "The true painter is the one in whom imagination speaks before all else" (*Journal,* II, 85).

30. *Recollections,* p. 62 (translation corrected; the last word is "it" [the chariot], not "him"). Already Roger de Piles had written: "Although his imagination was fertile, and although there is a vast array of objects present in his works, yet he did not let himself be overwhelmed by them" (Quoy que son imagination fût féconde, et que les objets s'y présentassent en foule, il ne s'en laissoit néanmoins pas accabler) in *Dissertation sur les ouvrages des plus fameux peintres* (Paris, 1681), p. 41; see George P. Mras, "Literary Sources of Delacroix's Conception of the Sketch and the Imagination," *Art Bulletin,* XLIV (1962), 103ff, esp. 110.

31. *Recollections,* p. 24.

32. E. Maurer, *Jacob Burckhardt und Rubens* (Basel, 1951), pp. 285ff.

Index